Retrospectives for Organizational Change

An Agile Approach

Jutta Eckstein

Retrospectives for Organizational Change

An Agile Approach

Jutta Eckstein

ISBN 978-3-947991-00-6

Cover design: Katja Gloggengießer, www.grellgelb.de

All pictures by Jutta Eckstein

URL of the book for updates etc.: https://www.jeckstein.com/retrospectives-for-organizational-change/

Also By Jutta Eckstein

Diving For Hidden Treasures

Company-wide Agility with Beyond Budgeting, Open Space & Sociocracy

Agile Software Development in the Large

Agile Software Development with Distributed Teams

Contents

Abbreviations . . . . **i**

List of Figures . . . . **iii**

Acknowledgments . . . . **v**

1. Preface **1**

2. Introduction **3**

3. Objective **7**

4. Design and Function of Retrospectives . **11**
    4.1   Duration, Participation, Attitude 13
    4.2   Purpose 15
    4.3   Phases 17

5. Challenges in Organizational Change . . **21**
    5.1   Different Kinds of Change 23
    5.2   Unclear Goals 26
    5.3   Increase in Demand for Participation . 29

6. Enabling Organizational Change **33**
    6.1   Diversity in Participation 35
    6.2   Existing Experiences 37
    6.3   Deciding What to Do 39

6.4 Relation and Demarcation to other Methods 40

7. Heuristic Evidence **45**
7.1 Usefulness for Change Management . . 46
7.2 Adaptive Action and Retrospectives . . 48

8. Experiences with Exemplary Applications 53
8.1 Feedback on the Meta-Level 54
8.2 Enabling Complex Change 57
8.3 Enabling Dynamic Change 61

9. Reflection on the Suggested Method . . . **65**

10. Closing Remarks **69**

Reference List **73**

Appendix **79**
Results from Open Space at RfG 2012/13 . . 80
Protocol of Workshop at XP 2013 90
Protocol of Enabling a Dynamic Change . . . 98
Protocol of Enabling a Complex Change . . . 110

About the Author **125**

Other Books by the Authors **129**

Index **135**

Abbreviations

cf.: confer (Latin), compare

e.g.: exempli gratia (Latin), for example

HSD: Human Systems Dynamics

ibid.: ibidem (Latin), the same place

i.e.: id est (Latin), that is

Kindle ed.: Kindle Edition

pos.: Position in ebook

PMO: Project Management Office

RfG: Retrospective Facilitator Gathering

XP: International Conference on Agile Software Development

List of Figures

Analysis while Playing (own illustration)

Landscape Diagram (cf. Holladay & Quade, 2008, p. 30)

Applicability of Concepts and Tools over Time (own illustration)

Relation to Adaptive Action (own illustration)

Tools and Techniques supporting Adaptive Action (own illustration)

Same and Different (own illustration)

Acknowledgments

This work would not have been possible without the contribution and feedback of my colleagues at the Retrospective Facilitators Gatherings in 2012 and 2013. I want to express my special gratitude to Diana Larsen who was brave enough to co-present this experimental topic at the XP conference in 2013. Additionally, I want to thank my clients from all over the world with whom I had the pleasure to work and learn with – not least about using Retrospective for Enabling Organizational Change.

Particularly, I want to acknowledge all the reviewers who provided their insights and feedback. Thanks to Kerstin Bücher and Nicolai M. Josuttis from Germany, Vikram Kapoor from the Netherlands, Charlotte Malther from Denmark, and to Diana Larsen and Linda Rising from the USA.

Finally I want to thank my professors from the University of Applied Sciences in Hamburg –Dr. Gernot Graeßner and Dr. Frank Strikker– for widening my horizon.

1. Preface

It is only the reader,
who turns a book into a book,
by reading it.

– Francis Ponge

It is recognizable how change becomes a natural companion of our daily work. This has and had as well an effect on the way I am working. That is the reason why I decided to go back to university in 2011 and go through a master's program in business coaching and change management. I plainly wanted to improve my skills in supporting the individual, the different teams, and the organization in succeeding in these turbulent times.

One of the "tools" I am using for a long time are retrospectives – yet only in the last maybe five years their real power became clear to me. Retrospectives leverage experiences of individuals for the better of the whole organization. Thus, it is not only to learn from past mistakes as a team but even more so for preparing for the future. How this can possibly work is the core of the book and was –at the same time– the focal point of my master thesis. This is the reason why this book has a deeper theoretical foundation than the other books I wrote. However, knowing

more about the effectiveness and the potency of
something helps as well to adjust it to own needs.
Additionally to the theoretical foundation, I included
a lot of material on real life experiences which
provide a counterbalance to the theory.

I hope you will find this book useful. I invite you
to explore the application of Retrospectives for Organizational Change, to visit the book's website
at: http://jeckstein.com/retrospectives[1] and to provide feedback on your experiences at: retrospec-
tives@jeckstein.com.

– Jutta Eckstein
April, 2014
Braunschweig, Germany

---

[1] http://jeckstein.com/retrospectives

2. Introduction

Now from memory experience is produced in men;
for the several memories of the same thing
produce finally the capacity for a single experience.

– Aristotle

Originally retrospectives, a special kind of a facilitated workshop for gaining feedback (German: Feedbackmoderation, cf. Graeßner, 2008, p. 156-168), have been designed to mainly look back at a finished (software) project and learn from these past experiences. The originator of retrospectives, Norm Kerth clarified that:

> "[r]etrospective rituals are more than just a review of the past. They also provide a chance to look forward, to plot the next project, and to plan explicitly what will be approached differently next time." (Kerth, 2001, p. 5)

Even with this forward looking perspective, retrospectives were still used as a ritual for finalizing a project and preparing for the next one. The usage of retrospectives changed with a new approach in software development: Agile software development, as defined by the Agile Manifesto[1] is based on a value system and twelve principles which emphasize the importance of collaboration, frequent feedback and continuous learning. The last principle of the Agile Manifesto[2] even requests the following:

> *"At regular intervals, the team reflects on how to become more effective, then tunes and adjusts its behavior accordingly."*

Thus, with the iterative approach of this kind of development it soon became common to not only reflect on the lessons learned at the end of a project, but both earlier and more regularly during the project. As a consequence, retrospectives are meanwhile well accepted in agile software development. The motivation for reflecting more frequently was according to Esther Derby and Diana Larsen that:

> *"[...] teams no longer wait until the end of a long project to inspect and adapt. They look for ways to improve at the end of every iteration." (Derby & Larsen, 2006, p. xx)*

Retrospectives are nowadays mainly used on a frequent basis in order to leverage the learning throughout a project. Most teams define this frequency as two weeks, some as one week others as one month. Yet still, the core idea of all these more or less frequent retrospectives is to reflect on a past

---

[1] http://agilemanifesto.org
[2] http://agilemanifesto.org/principles.html

common experience over a fixed period of time, to learn from this and to come up with ideas on what to do differently in the upcoming timeframe. Retrospectives allow a group to address changing needs through continuous learning and adaptation.

However, a group implementing this retrospective approach does not work in isolation. It is embedded in a greater whole – the organization. Yet, the organization that provides this environment faces many different challenges these days. Current trends suggest that approaches that enabled organizational changes in the past will not be successful in the future (cf. Scharmer, 2009, pos. 81). This suggests the need for organizations to look for change methods that address the current challenges, such as globalization or the growing demand in serious participation of everyone involved in the change (cf. Whitmore, 1996, p. 24).

3. Objective

The knowledge about the objective implies the urge for the objective.

– Oswald Spengler

The power of retrospectives shall be used in order to enable organizational change. Instead of building on the past experience of a completed iteration or project, the current diverse experiences of everyone involved or affected by the change shall be used to come up with and enable a necessary change. The involved persons will not necessarily share a common history, but a joint future. The idea is to stress, leverage and acknowledge the diverse histories (and therefore the different experiences) and use these as the basis for defining the future change.

A retrospective as a derivative of a facilitated workshop for gaining feedback provides then as well according to Gernot Graeßner:

> " [...] a review of the past, yet with the objective to learn for the future and to draw corresponding conclusions. The procedure can be regarded as part of a 'planning loop' and thus connects completed processes with a conscious affirmation of the

status quo or, more likely with the creation of new ideas for the future." (Graeßner, 2008, p. 166)

The emphasis for a Retrospective for Enabling Organizational Change is mainly on developing new ideas for the future, and less on completed processes. But it differs from a facilitated workshop for developing something new (German: Erarbeitungs¬moderation, cf. ibid., p. 105-116), by building on the existing experiences. As Graeßner explains, such a facilitated workshop takes experiences into account in two ways (cf. ibid., p. 109):

1. Experiences as a source for how to approach topics or problems.
2. Experiences that are made jointly during the facilitated workshop.

The Retrospectives for Organizational Change should reach beyond this two-fold consideration of experiences by founding the facilitated workshop on the existing individual experiences and using these for agreeing on what needs to persist and what needs to change. Although not common, experiences are still at the core of the Retrospective for Enabling Organizational Change and acknowledging them is what should make the change possible. This is in line with Gratton's assessment that experiences are at the fundamental core for shaping the future (cf. Gratton, 2011, pos. 4714).

The goal for this work is to analyze how different experiences can be leveraged for enabling a change using a retrospective approach. This analysis will remain on a conceptual level. As a result, elaborating on facilitation techniques that support such an approach are out of scope for this work.

4. Design and Function of Retrospectives

In effect, one knows,
whatever it is,
only long after one has learned it.

– Joseph Joubert

Retrospectives are well known by other names, in many different disciplines. For example, the army has used after-action-reviews for some time in order to understand the events of the last conflict and make vital corrections (cf. Senge et.al., 1999, p. 470-477). Coaches in professional sports conduct debriefs with their athletes to provide feedback and make necessary adjustments for the next challenge. For instance, American Football practices this to an extreme, in addition to the concept of time-out as known in other sports each move is analyzed while the game is going on.

Analysis while Playing (own illustration)

For example in the figure above, while the defensive team plays on the field (shown in the top left of the picture), the coach reflects with the offensive team on the last drive and discusses options and improvements for the next drive (presented at the bottom right of the picture). This crosses the boundary of the two knowledge types for capacity building –reflection on action and reflection in action (cf. Scharmer, 2009, pos. 6687-6691).

In the business world, software and other projects make often use of post-mortem or lessons learned sessions, especially for learning from a failure. Particularly in the software field, for more than ten years it has become a habit to retrospect regularly during the execution of a project, not only at the end (comparable to American Football). The reason is to learn from failure quickly and make corrections while it is still possible to do so. This way retrospectives foster continuous learning and improvement. Whereas at the end of the project, the team can indeed learn for the next project, but there is no way applying the lessons learned to the previous project.

Still, retrospectives as they are used right now are a means to reflect on a past timeframe. This timeframe can be a finalized project –no matter if successful or not–, a phase of a project, or a period of a joint collaboration of an organizational unit. Thus in general, a retrospective always examines a defined timeframe and focuses on lessons learned from it.

4.1 Duration, Participation, Attitude

The duration of a retrospective depends on the lengths of the time period under examination, the complexity of the project, the team's size, and the potential for conflict within the team (cf. Derby & Larsen, 2006, p. 17-18). For example, analyzing a whole project takes one to three days, whereas regular retrospectives that are scheduled every two weeks as it is typical for agile software development are as short as forty-five minutes to two hours (cf. ibid. and Kerth, 2001, p. 53-55). However, the duration is not standardized.

Everyone involved should take part in the session.[1] Moreover, including the different perspectives ensures everyone has a say in what changes need to happen in the future. Naomi Karten emphasizes the importance of this as follows:

"Inviting people to have a say makes them feel valued. It generates valuable ideas,

---

[1] Participation and physical attendance in a retrospective can be challenging and has to be carefully addressed if the project team is extremely large and/or globally distributed (cf. Eckstein, 2004, p. 102-111 and Eckstein, 2010, p. 151-166). However, this is out of scope for this work.

particularly from people who have a deeper understanding of how the change will affect their work than those leading the change. And it has the power to transform resistance into wholehearted support. In times of change, people want to have a say." *(Karten, 2009, p. 124)*

This approach also has a democratic aspect, because it is not a manager deciding what kind of lesson needs to be learned, it is the whole team creating that knowledge together.

Yet in order to ensure joint knowledge creation, the attitude of the participants in the retrospective is crucial. Especially when looking at past experiences, it is likely that people will start explaining themselves and look for someone who was in charge and who could be blamed for whatever went wrong. However, this attitude is not helpful. What is needed instead is an open mindset to learn from the past with a focus on aspiration and hope for the future (cf. Whitmore, 1996, p. 25). The so-called prime directive of retrospectives defines this attitude as such:

"Regardless of what we discover we must understand and truly believe that everyone did the best job he or she could, given what was known at the time, his or her skills and abilities, the resources available, and the situation at hand." *(Kerth, 2001, p. 7)*

At the beginning of the session, the participants clarify and agree on this common attitude. Most often the prime directive is visible on a poster throughout the session. This prohibits finger-pointing in the team and ensures the general understanding that it is quite normal that hindsight is a wonderful thing.

4.2 Purpose

Learning from experiences and continuously improving are at the core of retrospectives. This is especially important these days, because competition –caused by globalization– is tougher, and the pressure on individuals and teams is stronger. As Senge et.al. explain:

> "If anything, our work and personal lives have become more fragmented in recent years, with increasing workloads, stress, and compromises to personal and family values." (Senge et.al., 1999, p. 47)

The increasing fragmentation leads to permanent action, which means that people rarely take time to stop and reflect on what is really helping and what is hindering, including existing norms and policies. Yet, only this kind of reflection makes real learning possible (cf. Argyris & Schön, 1978, p. 139). Retrospectives are a means for implementing a regular pause for reflection as part of the company's culture. This reflection helps to stop the treadmill of ineffective actions (Stacey, 2011, p. 5). According to Kerth, retrospectives do not only provide support to improve the process guiding all actions, yet they also foster personal development. Learning from experience provides a way for every individual to learn, grow and mature (cf. Kerth, 2001, p. xvi). In order to do so, retrospectives focus on both – possibilities for improvement and recognizing what went well. Collecting both kind of information helps each individual to understand his or her own contribution.

Bringing all people together, who were involved in the timeframe under examination, allows seeing and understanding the big picture: What has happened (and what needs to happen next). As Kerth points out:

> *"This big-picture wisdom comes from our ability to understand the relationship between an individual's work and that of the entire team. We need to tell our piece and see how it helps make up the whole story."* (ibid., p. 5)

Without a facilitated workshop like a retrospective, the risk is high that individuals do not understand their contribution to the bigger picture and thus take actions that are not in-line with the direction of the intent. So, a retrospective contributes additional to the understanding of each individual's role in the larger, organizational, context:

> *"Each member of the organization constructs his or her own representation, or image, of the theory-in-use of the whole. That picture is always incomplete. The organization members strive continually to complete it,*

and to understand themselves in the con-
text of the organization." (Argyris & Schön,
1978, p. 16)

Understanding the whole story allows deep insights for lessons learned from the past undertaking. Therefore, through understanding the big picture, the purpose of a retrospective is –as requested by the last principle of the Agile Manifesto– to allow first and foremost single-loop learning by inviting the team to adjust its behavior in order to get more effective (cf. Chapter Introduction and Argyris & Schön, 1978, p. 18-20). Yet, if the team uses the retrospectives additionally for examining the support and effect of (organizational) norms on its own behavior also double-loop learning is happening (cf. ibid., p. 20-26). Moreover, retrospectives can enable deutero-learning if the individuals reflect on their own interactions and hence start to learn how they learn (cf. ibid., p. 26-28 and p. 102).

4.3 Phases

A retrospective is defined by five phases, which compare to Seifert's six phases of a facilitation cycle (cf. Derby & Larsen, 2006, p. 5-14 compared to Seifert, 2011, pos. 443-530). Below the five retrospective phases are listed and briefly explained with Seifert's pendants stated in parenthesis:

1. **Set the Stage** (comparable to *introduction*): In addition to welcoming everyone and enabling

not only the physical but also the mental presence of all participants, opening the workshop, clarifying all organizational issues and working agreements, this phase focuses on ensuring a safe environment. Only the latter enables everyone to speak openly and honestly.

2. **Gather Data** (comparable to *collect topics*): This phase concentrates on the "retro"-part of the retrospective. The participants collect data on events, hard facts (like operating profits), perceptions, beliefs, and results of the past timeframe under examination.

3. **Generate Insights:** The team analyzes and discusses the collected data and looks for themes, patterns, puzzles, or lessons by sometimes challenging each other's perspective.

4. **Decide what to do** (comparable to *select and work on topics* as well as to *action planning*): The team makes additional investigations into the outcomes of the insights. They decide on the insights they want to work on further. Then they elaborate on these topics and come up with an action plan. Finally the team offers a commitment to the things they want to act on in the upcoming timeframe.

5. **Close the retrospective** (comparable to *closing*): In the last phase, the team focuses on the transfer of the retrospective results (e.g. how to track the committed action plan, or how to document the results), on offering appreciations for all participants' efforts and on gathering feedback on the retrospective itself.

Particularly if performed frequently, the power of the retrospective results from regular self-reflection of the team and its continuous search for improvement.

5. Challenges in Organizational Change

Change is necessary
Like the renewal of the leaves in spring.

– Vincent van Gogh

In 1978, Argyris and Schön described the increasing need for organizations to deal with the instability and changes going on both in the internal and external environment (cf. Argyris & Schön, 1978, p. 125). Since then, the challenges organizations face have been amplified. Nowadays, organizational change has many implications:

- Change is happening continuously and is never a single occurrence. Different from what Kurt Lewin once assumed that there is time to unfreeze, change, and refreeze a situation or a process, now change is a continuous process (cf. Lewin, 1947). Moreover, many changes are happening in parallel and at high speed. Therefore, it is not helpful to use the same approach for addressing a change now as for one in the past. As Kotter summarizes:
  „Firms that try to juggle twenty change projects

today by using the methods that successful companies applied to the same problem three decades ago always seem to fail." (Kotter, 2012, pos. 1972 / p. 147)[1]

- Analysis of cause and effect is not effective anymore. The main reason is that things are interdependent and there is rarely one cause that can be singled out and declared as the reason for a specific effect. It is possible to fail when searching for a single cause only (cf. Eoyang, 2009, p. 46). Zimmerman, Lindberg, and Plsek elaborate on this by pointing out that organizations are complex adaptive systems and as such can be characterized as follows:

  „[Complex adaptive systems] have a number of linked attributes or properties. Because all the attributes are linked, it is impossible to identify the starting point for the list of attributes. Each one can be seen to be both a cause and effect of the other attributes." (Zimmerman, Lindberg & Plsek, 2008, p. 8)

- This means there are almost always many different interrelated causes that lead to a specific circumstance.
- There is no relation in magnitude between a problem and a solution. For example, a small change can make no difference, a moderate difference, or a huge difference. Gleick summarizes this as:

  „Tiny differences in input could quickly become overwhelming differences in output [...] this translates into what is only half-jokingly known

---

[1] Whenever the ebook supports page numbers, I provide them additionally. According to the ebook seller these page numbers correspond to the print version of the book.

as the Butterfly Effect–the notion that a butter-fly stirring the air today in Peking can transform storm systems next month in New York ." (Gle-ick, 2011, pos. 155-161 / p. 8)

Internal factors may drive organizational changes, yet more so additional influencers like the five (external) forces: need for low-carbon economy, changes in demography, advances in technology, increased globalization, and changes in society. These five forces influence the necessary changes as well as how these changes can be carried out. The interrelationship of these forces and the necessary changes lead to a high complexity (cf. Gratton, 2011, pos. 267-275).

5.1 Different Kinds of Change

Depending on the challenge, an organization must decide what kind of change strategy fits best. In order to do, there must be a clear understanding of the different change options available. Addressing a necessary change with the wrong strategy will most likely lead to failure. Eoyang and Holladay explain the three different kinds of change (cf. Eoyang & Holladay, 2013, pos. 1044-1198 / p. 53-62):

1. **Static change:** A static change assumes that both the current state and the future state are well known. Accordingly, the only thing needed is the transition from the current to the future state (cf. Beckhard & Pritchard, 1992, p. 14).

This means that this kind of change is both predictable and controllable. The change strategy involves mainly a thorough planning and verification effort. The recommended methods for this kind of change are traditional root-cause analysis with consequent problem solving, application of best (or good) practices, Lewin's change model of unfreeze-change-refreeze (cf. Lewin, 1947, p. 34-36) or expert judgment.

2. **Dynamic change:** A dynamic change pretends that the future state –or the goal– is predictable. However, it is unclear how the goal can be reached. It is most likely that there is no direct path toward the goal, so there is the need to meander ahead. Most often, this kind of change requires a stepwise approach, where each step will be taken according its alignment with the goal. Following strict rules is a hindrance. Therefore, it is preferable to adjust and adapt. Typical change methods supporting this strategy are planned change initiatives, leading change step-by-step (cf. Kotter, 2012), the application of expert processes and leadership and/or employee development plans.

3. **Complex change** (also known as dynamical change): This change is regarded as complex, because neither the future state is clear nor the path toward it. As a result, this kind of change is viewed as emergent, highly unstable, and unpredictable. The only way to deal with a complex change is to iterate. Thus, actions are performed incrementally and the outcome is examined for emerging patterns that provide more clarity about both the goal and the direction toward it. This strategy is supported by the

following change methods: Action Learning (cf. Revans, 2011), double-loop learning (cf. Argyris & Schön, 1978), Adaptive Action (cf. Eoyang & Holladay, 2013), or Cynefin (cf. Kurtz & Snowden, 2003).

Scharmer regards these three kinds of change as complexities organizations face. For him, a static change is defined as dynamic complexity, because the cause is detached from the effect either by space and/or by time. Dynamic change is regarded as social complexity defined by conflicting world-views by different stakeholders. And finally, complex change is seen as emergent complexity, because disruption and continuous changes make it impossible to predict a future state (cf. Scharmer, 2009, pos. 3682). However, the main problem is that most complex organizational challenges are treated as if the necessary change would be static or dynamic. As Eoyang and Holladay explain:

> *"Sometimes we think of change in human systems as if it were static change. From this perspective, we expect easy transitions from pre-strategic plan to post-strategic plan; bad employee to good employee; expectation to outcome; unproductive team to productive team; toxic culture to generative culture. Of course, change seldom really happens this way [...]" (Eoyang & Holladay, 2013, pos. 454 / p. 22)*

Most often, the change is complex and therefore needs a different approach. However, it is difficult to start a change initiative with an unclear goal.

5.2 Unclear Goals

The unpredictability of the goal is on the one hand based on the five forces and on the other hand determined by both high uncertainty and disagreement in the organization. The relationship between the latter two factors is expressed by the so-called Landscape Diagram (cf. Holladay & Quade, 2008, p. 29-41 and presented in the following figure).

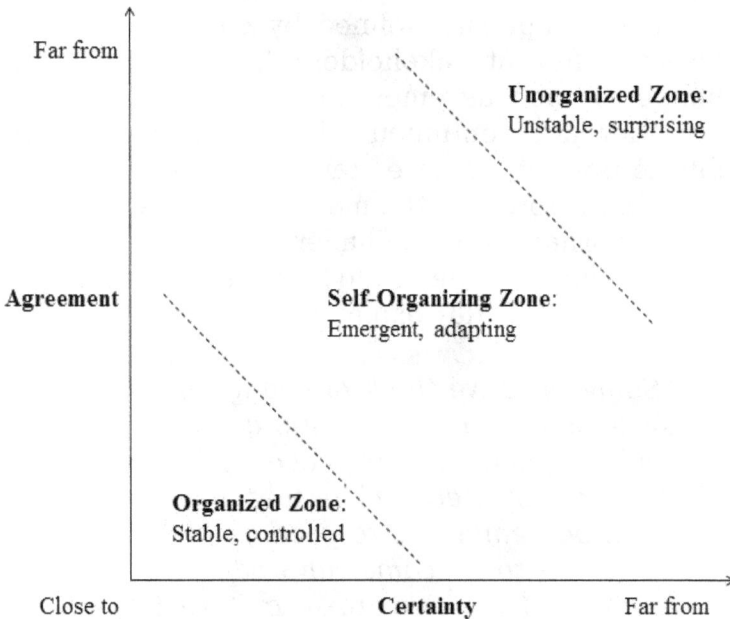

Landscape Diagram (cf. Holladay & Quade, 2008, p. 30)

Stacey developed this diagram based on the relationship between a change context and the way decisions are made (cf. Stacey, 1996, p. 47). Before Holladay and Quade developed this model further, it was Zimmerman, Lindberg, and Plsek who refined it by creating the Stacey agreement and certainty matrix (cf. Zimmerman, Lindberg & Plsek, 2008, p. 136-143).

The Landscape Diagram visualizes decision-making. Every decision is driven by the certainty about the issue under consideration and by how much the group is in agreement with respect to this issue. Both of these factors –certainty and agreement– drive the decision toward or away from the (change) goal and this way define the conclusion. The degree of certainty and agreement determines on a "zone" that applies. For example, if everyone is in agreement and absolutely certain then the organized zone applies, which is defined by a stable and controlled environment. If there is no agreement and everyone is completely uncertain about the situation, then the unorganized zone applies. This is determined by instability and many surprises. In between, there is the self-organizing zone, which classified emergence and adaptation.

Yet, no situation is attached to a specific zone, which means that no particular strategy is generally advisable as the following example shows (cf. Holladay & Quade, 2008, p. 32):

- Research and development are for instance undertakings that happen typically in an **unorganized zone**, because there is no clear goal. Therefore, creativity, exploration, and experimentation are important in order to discover the goal.
- As soon as research and development has more clarity about the goal, the approach shifts toward the **self-organizing zone**. Now, the work

is focused around creating prototypes and per-
haps a plan for further examination of the goal.
- Once the prototypes have proven the attrac-
tiveness and practicality of the goal, the whole
effort will shift to the **organized zone**. What
was at first research and development will now
turn into production, which means that rules
and regulations apply.

Generally, as constraints are increased, e.g. by introducing strict rules, every issue moves to a more
organized area because it shifts certainty and agreement (and vice versa). In the past, only one of the two
factors had been challenging – uncertainty. Agreement was no issue, because hardly anyone cared
about it. As long as the top manager was certain
about the goal, the whole organization would have
worked for it. Yet, this does not create much support
necessarily as Holman, Devane, and Cady point out:

> *"When strategic direction is merely passed
> down from the top of the organization or
> from governmental officials, often there is
> mi¬ni¬mal understanding of the strategic
> details and related assumptions because
> only select people were present during strat-
> egy development. With the use of whole
> system change methods, typically more peo-
> ple are involved in setting the strategy and
> therefore understand the nuances and rea-
> sons for selected options." (Holman, De-
> vane & Cady, 2007, p. 6)*

As Holman, Devane, and Cady explain above, including the whole system in the change ensures under-

standing and agreement, which in turn generates more certainty.

5.3 Increase in Demand for Participation

In the past most decisions about future changes have been made top-down by the corporation. Yet, hierarchical command structures and top-down decision-making diminish as the major leadership style and give way wider employee participation (cf. Seddon, 2003 and Gratton, 2011, pos. 4708). Bill Brenneman explains why:

> *"Aside from being open to abuse, this 'command-and-control' model of hierarchy is a poor path to high performance in contemporary industrial settings. [...] A strong focus on accountability and stewardship provides an antidote to 'command-and-control' abuses of power." (Brenneman in Senge et.al., 1999, p. 388)*

Additionally, command-and-control as a leadership style is not regarded as the most effective one, because only when employees are convinced about a goal will they be motivated to achieve it. This is based on the emotional attachment that is created by meaningful involvement (cf. Holman, Devane & Cady, 2007, p. 6).

Yet, participation and involvement are still not the state-of-the-art in industry as Bjarte Bogsnes points out:

> *"It is quite a paradox how 'western' busi-*
> *ness leaders praise democracy as the obvi-*
> *ous and undisputable model for how to or-*
> *ganize society effectively. When the same*
> *leaders turn to their own companies, then*
> *their beliefs and inspiration seem to come*
> *from a very different place, from the very*
> *opposite ideologies." (Bogsnes, 2008, pos.*
> *392)*

But still, democracy is spreading – in the world by more and more countries asking for public partic- ipation[2] and in industry with employees' requests for understanding and meaning making of the pro- cesses inside the company. The latter request has many roots. Jeremy Rifkin observes that the younger, well-educated generation is not ready to accept fixed social norms; instead they value transparency, joint action, and equal relationships (cf. Rifkin, 2011, p. 27). Hence, young professionals in the next gener- ation are not willing to accept the existing organi- zational structures. They mostly grew up without hierarchies compared to earlier generations who participated in Boy Scouts or church groups. The new generation is used to questioning goals and approaches, and to self-organizing in networks as appropriate. That is why, according to Rifkin, we are currently seeing a shift from vertical power (expressed in hierarchies) to a lateral one that au- thorizes people through network structures (ibid., p. 13).

To be successful, an organization needs to ensure

---

[2]The request for public participation became transparent e.g. in Ger- many during the Stuttgart 21 protests.

that employees understand the necessary changes, the uncertainty and disagreement regarding the goals, and that they are continuously part of the learning process.

6. Enabling Organizational Change

Everyone can learn from the past.
Today it depends on whether one can learn from the future.

– Herman Kahn

Retrospectives for Organizational Change are structurally the same as classical retrospectives. For example, the phases and the attitude expressed through the prime directive stay intact (cf. Chapter 3.1 and 2.3). Although the general course of action remains the same, it is mainly the purpose of the three middle phases that shifts. Conversely this means, the first and the last phase –setting the stage and closing the retrospective– stay the same.

The result of a classical retrospective that examines a whole project or just a phase of it is typically a change for the team. Very often, these are small but important course corrections in terms of processes, communication, or technological collaboration that the team can accomplish in the upcoming timeframe (cf. Derby & Larsen, 2006, p. 148). However, these kinds of changes are not the focal point here. The first difference is that participants in a Retrospective for Enabling Organizational Change do not examine a specific timeframe. The second difference is that they most often do not share a common history and as a consequence do not form a team.

What brings them together is the idea that something needs to change. Sometimes they already know what needs to change, but they are uncertain about how, which is a classical situation for a dynamic change. Sometimes even the goal for the change is unclear or there is no agreement on it, which means the group faces a complex change. The Landscape Diagram can be visualized as an area on the floor and used as a set up for a group constellation by asking each member to stand in the zone that reflects best his or her certainty and agreement with the goal. This can help during a Retrospective for Enabling Organizational Change to get more clarity about the objective, by making transparent what is obvious and necessary for one group member but not for another one (cf. Senge et.al., 2011, pos. 2225). The Landscape Diagram can be used as such during all of the following phases as clarity and agreement disappear: gather data, generating insight, or decide what to do. For enabling just a static change, such a retrospective would most likely be not cost-efficient (speaking primarily of investing time). Yet, for a dynamic and even more so for a complex change it is a method that can help to identify the goal and how to approach it. Moreover, using such kind of retrospectives regularly during the change process allows verifying if the goal and/or the path toward it are still valid.

The reflective part is very important in this session

because it allows the gathering of all the experiences of those in the room and to learn from them.

6.1 Diversity in Participation

No matter what kind of change is introduced, based on today's challenges for organizations it will always be important to ensure participation from people with different perspectives. As Lynda Gratton emphasizes:

> "[...] collections of people with diverse perspectives and ways of seeing the world can rapidly outperform collections of people who rely on a single perspective." (Gratton, 2011, pos. 2309-2315)

Both the goal and the approach toward the change will be created and verified from all the different perspectives. So on the one hand, the diversity of the group improves the change. But, more important, on the other hand all the people representing these different views will feel ownership of the change and at the same time recognizing that they will benefit from it. Holman, Devane, and Cady point out that when people recognize that their opinion is valued, they take responsibility (Holman, Devane & Cady, 2007, p. 12). Moreover, in order to make a difference, people choose to take responsibility and be accountable for implementing the change (cf. Whitmore, 1996, p. 25).

Understanding different perspectives has the additional effect of seeing the whole story of the diverse opportunities the change can provide. Originally, the importance of big-picture wisdom has been emphasized when examining a past timeframe (cf. Chapter 3.2), yet it is equally important when designing the future. Sharing experiences from different projects, functional roles, departments, or even organizations supports collaborative learning. Bunker and Alban stress this:

> *"Listening to other perspectives, often for the first time, while exploring the environmental context before problem solving or positioning moves people from 'Me and my view' to 'What are we going to do about this?' From this dialogue a new picture of the future can emerge." (Bunker & Alban, 2007, pos. 6644)*

Bringing different perspectives together is a precondition for initiating a change, as Stacey points out:

> *"Systems in which the entities and their interactions are all the same cannot spontaneously generate anything new." (Stacey, 2011, p. 92)*

Stacey moreover emphasizes that any kind of change emerges through conversations. Gathering people in a Retrospective for Enabling Organizational Change ensures that these conversations are happening. Additionally, allowing the change goal to emerge during such a retrospective is according to Stacey the only way that permits change to happen, because the themes around a change occur through conversations (ibid., p. 365). This is similar to Scharmer's understanding that only the relationships among individuals make new things possible (cf. Scharmer, 2009, pos. 3514-3516).

6.2 Existing Experiences

A foundation for every kind of change is to acknowledge existing experiences and to clarify what should remain stable – despite all changes. Often, by collecting existing experiences it becomes obvious to the group what sort of patterns define a kind of "organizational DNA" for the company. According to Senge et.al., the organizational DNA is defined by i.e. past accomplishments and strengths and therefore provides a foundation for future changes (cf. Senge et.al., 2011, pos 4804-4809). Just as the DNA of family members marks self-similarity, so does the DNA of a company (cf. Eoyang, 2009, p. 71). Although the individuals (of either a family or an organization) differ, they still display similarities. For family members this is foremost visually detectable (i.e. similar facial features) whereas for employees this becomes apparent through behavioral patterns. Changing the DNA of an organization might mean destroying its key strength. Related to a similar concept named organizational fractals, Eoyang stated:

"The common idea lends coherence to the organization, because it provides an underlying similarity to all corporate actions. It

*provides for some form of predictability,
even in the face of constantly changing
circumstances. It sets a reliable context in
which all corporate and business decisions
can be made." (ibid., p. 68)*

Thus, during the Retrospective for Enabling Organizational Change the approach of first gathering data or rather first collecting the different experiences is the most important step. It ensures that there is no manager propagating the change and telling people what to do. It is instead respecting the wisdom of everyone involved and using this wisdom for letting the best change possible emerge. Additionally, acknowledging existing experiences makes it easier for people involved to accept the change. Ignoring experiences often triggers the impression, that everything done in the past has been wrong which leads to clinging even more to the old way of doing things (cf. Derby & Larsen, 2006, p. 149). As a consequence, although the participants of a Retrospective for Enabling Organizational Change do not share a common time period, it is still important that they bring together their individual experiences.

Gaining insights into existing experiences allows understanding the strengths and weaknesses of the situation at hand. Yet, this will only work, if the involved people are diverse. Otherwise the insights created will only be one-sided and not really useful.

6.3 Deciding What to Do

The Butterfly Effect should be taken into account when deciding on what should be done. Nobody knows in advance what kind of action has what kind of effect, as Gribbin states:

> „The same size triggers do not all cause the same size events." (Gribbin, 2004, pos. 2759-2765)

As a consequence, it is no longer necessary to focus on the most pressing and difficult problem first, because solving a tiny (and at first glance less important) problem might have the biggest effect. Malcolm Gladwell assembled even a whole book sharing stories about what he calls *The Tipping Point: How Little Things Can Make a Big Difference* (cf. Gladwell, 2000). The little things Gladwell is referring to are for example slight changes in the context, or in the way a change is communicated (cf. ibid., p. 166). Moreover, it is neither required that the whole organization nor the (top) management support the change, because a tiny change in one area can have a huge effect on the whole organization (cf. Eoyang & Holladay, 2013, pos. 4208 / p. 233). This is in-line with Scharmer's belief that the world is changeable with five people only (cf. Scharmer, 2009, pos. 6196).

In a Retrospective for Enabling Organizational Change the group focuses on changes that can be implemented easily and evaluates a few weeks later –

in the next retrospective– if these changes made a difference.

This provides the additional consequence of achieving early wins which motivate proceeding with the change initiative. Therefore, it is both a reward for those who worked on the early wins and a justification for the change (cf. Kotter, 2012, pos. 1635-1836 / p. 121-135).Whereas concentrating on the most difficult issue first, might lead to exhausting people or to failure.

6.4 Relation and Demarcation to other Methods

Similar methods to Retrospectives for Organizational Change exist. Likewise these methods focus on initiating and implementing change while building on the experiences of the participants. First and foremost Action Learning, the Action Review Cycle, Futurespective, and Organizational Learning Cycle have to be named:

- **Action Learning** (cf. Holman, Devane & Cady, 2007, p. 479-483): This has been introduced by Revans and developed further by many others. The focus is on uncovering patterns by analyzing the experience of the participants through inquiry. Action Learning differentiates between peer coaching with participants from similar positions but different functional areas and team learning, where the session is conducted for an intact team. Similar to holding regular classical retrospectives, Action Learning is meant to be repeated in order to reflect and act. The main difference to the suggested method using retrospectives is in the participants: Retrospectives for Organizational Change can address as well peer groups or intact teams, yet its main focus is on participants from different functional areas across hierarchies, roles and responsibilities for ensuring a high diversity.

- **Action Review Cycle** (cf. Holman, Devane & Cady, 2007, p. 484-489): This is a combination of Before Action Review, where the participants focus on planning actions, the execution of the actions, and finally the After Action Review, where the actual results are examined and compared to the initial plan. This way, the Action Review Cycle concentrates on continuous learning and adjusting. This is closely related to the suggested retrospective approach, except that the Action Review Cycle is mainly action-driven and thus better comparable to classical yet more participative project management. The focus of Retrospectives for Organizational Change is not purely on actions (although this is often an outcome) but rather on the conversations, sharing of experiences, and emergence of ideas.
- **Futurespective** (cf. Kua, 2013, p. 81-83): A Futurespective is a variant of a classical retrospective and is slightly related to the future pacing of neurolinguistic programming (cf. Bandler & Grinder, 1975). It is especially designed for initiating a change. A Futurespective starts with creating a vision for the future and then derives insights, events, and actions to make the vision happen. The major difference to a

Retrospective for Organizational Change is that
a Futurespective does not focus on gathering
existing experiences it concentrates instead on
dreaming up a joint vision. In a Futurespective
the phases gathering data and generating insights are merely visionary. Only when deciding
what to do the participants come up with actions based on the envisioned insights. Although
a good method for generating a creative vision,
the Futurespective does neither acknowledge
the existing experiences within a group nor
does it deal with disagreements or uncertainties
regarding the goal.

- **Organizational Learning Cycle** (cf. Dixon &
Ross in Senge et.al., 1999, p. 435-444): The
model of the Organizational Learning Cycle con-
sists of four quadrants, which are continuously
repeated. It starts with *widespread generation
of information*, where people who are perform-
ing the action (rather than managers of the
actions) gather the information. The second
quadrant deals with *integration and dissemina-
tion*. The focus is here on understanding both
the big-picture of the organization and the individual interrelated parts of it. The third quadrant, called *collective interpretation* deals with
sense-making of all the information despite the
differences in assumptions. The final quadrant,
authority to take responsible action, stresses
that in order to act responsibly people have to
have the authority to make necessary changes.
The Organizational Learning Cycle is closely
related to the Retrospectives for Organizational
Change. The major difference is in the lack of
the reflection in the first quadrant. Only with

the start of the second round in the cycle people are asked to learn from the experiences of the last execution of the cycle. Thus, only the joint experiences made during the Organizational Learning Cycle are taken into account. Whereas the retrospectives' core lies in starting a change initiative with acknowledging the existing experiences.

Although there are related methods available, the coverage of the breadth and depth differs to the Retrospectives for Organizational Change. The biggest distinctions are the gathering of participants from different functional areas across hierarchies, roles and responsibilities as well as leveraging and acknowledging the diverse experiences right from the beginning.

Although, the general design with the five phases is the same for a Retrospective for Enabling Organizational Change as for a classical retrospective, the main differences are that the participants do not necessarily have a common history and there is no specific timeframe that will be examined. This changes the focus or rather the purpose of the three middle phases –gather data, generate insights, decide what to do– to some extent.

7. Heuristic Evidence

For only all too often something gets recognized without putting it into practice.

– Francesco Guicciardini

In the past two years I offered the topic on Retrospectives for Organizational Change at different conferences. One of them –the *Retrospective Facilitator Gathering (RfG)*[1] – is exclusively addressed to professional facilitators of retrospectives, who attend on personal invitation only, and is organized as an Open Space conference (cf. Harrison Owen in Holman, Devane & Cady, 2007, p. 135-148). It is as such the only conference worldwide focusing on retrospectives. I suggested the topic both in 2012 and 2013 see Appendix. In addition to developing the idea of Retrospectives for Organizational Change further, I wanted to see if the topic is of interest at all and if it has any potential. This has been confirmed by the participants in both years. The RfGs provided some feedback on the meta-level of the usefulness and applicability of Retrospectives for Organizational Change and additionally uncovered areas for further development.

---

[1] http://retrospectivefacilitatorgathering.org/

7.1 Usefulness for Change Management

When first discussing the topic at the RfG in 2012, the professional retrospective facilitators emphasized the distinction between how retrospectives serve as methods and how they philosophically or rather conceptually support change management.

As shown in the figure below we collected specific tools or general concepts and how these apply over time when using retrospectives for change management (using the x-axis for time). Placing the tools or concepts on a continuum (the y-axis in the figure) provided us a better understanding of the two different aspects of retrospectives in the context of change management: retrospectives as methods or as concepts. Using this visualization we discovered that for instance the following conceptual elements of retrospectives support its usage for change management:

- Uncovering organizational patterns to amplify or to change and identify change opportunities
- Understanding ourselves – the reasons why we do what we do
- Supporting complex adaptive systems change
- Focusing on organizational learning, where real learning equals individual change
- Creating a shared picture / goal and envision the desired future of the change
- Creating a supportive collaboration environment
- Collecting success stories and things to preserve in the change

- Evaluating the status of the change initiative –
where are we in the change (e.g. according to
Virginia Satir's change model, cf. Satir et.al.,
1991)

**Applicability of Concepts and Tools over Time (own illus-
tration)**

These findings were verified in the following year. In
2013 we focused more on the use of retrospectives

on the organizational level. There we discussed how
to engage a dedicated champion for the change,
prevent or mitigate resistance and why we believe
it is important to investigate further in this topic (cf.
Manns & Rising, 2005, p. 79-84 and p. 129-131).
In these discussions the professional retrospective
facilitators agreed that the suggested Retrospective
for Enabling Organizational Change is a method for:

- understanding the necessity of a change,
- including everyone,
- and getting insights within and about the organization.

This made us conclude, that retrospectives are def-
initely an instrument for enabling organizational
change.

7.2 Adaptive Action and Retrospectives

Another discussion that started at the RfG in 2012
was the relation of retrospectives to Adaptive Action
with respect to change management (cf. Eoyang
& Holladay, 2013). The core of Adaptive Action is
a learning cycle, which is defined by asking three
questions (see next figure)[2]:

1. **What**: This is asked in order to gather data,
   which defines both the entry point to and the

---

[2]The figure references HSD –Human Systems Dynamics– which is the
theory Adaptive Action supports.

closing from the last learning cycle. In a Retrospective for Enabling Organizational Change focusing on this question allows collecting and sharing the different experiences for initiating the change.

2. **So what**: The next question is *so what* – for generating insights on the collected data. As mentioned earlier, for understanding the big picture it is helpful if the group is diverse and many different perspectives are taken into account. One of the recommendations for this step was to perform a status check of the change by a comparison to the change phases (cf. Satir et.al., 1991).

3. **Now what**: The final question is *now what* – here the group decides what to do with all these insights. For ensuring that the action supports the general goal, we recommended for every action to first define a test that verifies the alignment with the goal. This has been stressed several times, because the professional retrospective facilitators have noticed that actions have been performed and worked, yet they did not support the goal (this oftentimes has only been discovered after the fact). Moreover, we found it important to focus on small actions. First of all, because a small action is easy to implement and might still have a huge effect. And second because achieving results early creates confidence in the change (cf. Manns & Rising, 2005, p. 216-218).

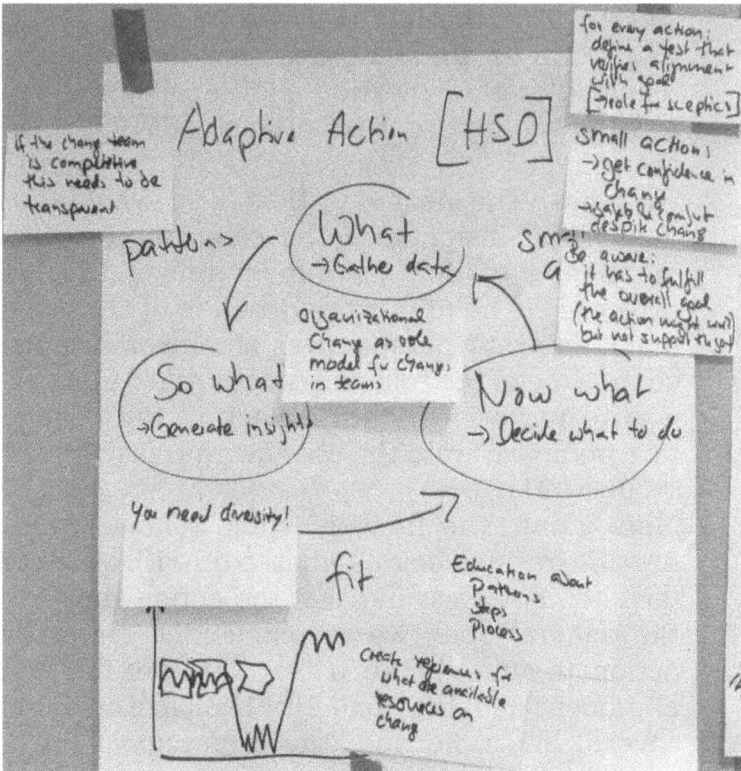

Relation to Adaptive Action (own illustration)

Entering the next learning cycle means again gathering data by asking once more *what* - now for reviewing the success of the planned actions and the experiments that have been performed as an outcome of the last *now what*.

For making the connection between retrospectives and Adaptive Action transparent, we collected tools and techniques used in retrospectives and categorized them according to the question they help to elaborate (see picture below)[3].

Tools and Techniques supporting Adaptive Action (own illustration)

The collection of tools and techniques for supporting the three questions was quite impressive. Yet,
it occurred to us that we are missing the piece
that helps close the circle from asking *now what*

---

[3]Although not all of the sticky notes are readable in the picture, it still
shows the close connection between retrospectives and Adaptive Action by
the pure amount of tools and techniques for the three questions.

in the first round to examining *what* in the next
round of Adaptive Action. Yet, it can as well be
discussed how important it is to close the circle
with tools and techniques, because between two
retrospectives only daily business and implementing
the change happens.

Still, thus far, we concentrated mainly on examining a specific time period, but did not pay much
attention to making the retrospective a sequence
supporting a greater whole. However, it was ev-
ident to us that retrospectives currently support
the feedback loop from the individual and his or
her personal experience to the awareness about the
greater whole by the interaction within the group
(cf. Scharmer, 2009, pos. 1011).

8. Experiences with Exemplary Applications

Nothing sinking so gently,
and so deep,
into men's minds,
as example.

– John Locke

At a conference focusing on agile software development, I conducted a session with people experienced in either facilitating of or participating in mostly frequent classical retrospectives.

Additionally, I collected experiences using Retrospectives for Organizational Change when helping my clients to initiating and implementing change. The change introduced was either a switch to agile software development, a change in the organizational structure or in organizational processes.

Although the session at the conference allowed discussions on the meta-level of the topic, all the sessions contributed to gaining experiences in applying Retrospectives for Organizational Change.

8.1 Feedback on the Meta-Level

At XP 2013[1], an international conference on agile software development, we brought the topic of Retrospective for Enabling Organizational Change to the attention of the audience.[2] Although six sessions were running in parallel, we were able to attract more than a quarter of the whole audience. The number of participants provided some feedback regarding the importance and timeliness of the topic.

The participants were all familiar with retrospectives in general. Hence, there was no need to explain the five phases of a retrospective, yet the relation to Adaptive Action was new to them. Therefore, we decided to use Adaptive Action as our structure for the session – for not only talking about it but letting the participants experience it cf. Appendix.

After introducing the topic, we asked participants to gather data in groups by answering *what* are their experiences in introducing a change and in using retrospectives for continuous improvement. After collecting some of the data in the plenary, we suggested that participants generate insights based on their own experiences. We did so by asking the groups to focusing on *so what* has supported or hindered introducing change and using retrospectives for improvement. For debriefing we asked them to come up with particularly difficult issues on the insights discussed. At this stage we offered some methods for generating insights, for example

---

[1] http://www.xp2013.org

[2] I conducted this session together with Diana Larsen – a retrospective facilitator colleague of mine.

we gave an introduction to the different kinds of change –static, dynamic, and complex– and to Adaptive Action (cf. Chapter 4.1 and Chapter 6.2). Both of these methods helped put the difficult issue (and the desired change) in perspective.

As the last step we focused on deciding what to do, by asking *now what* needs to be done. We used a difficult issue from one of the participants (which has been experienced by almost everyone in the audience) as an example for next possible steps. The example was at first stated as "project management regulations" and then detailed into differences and misunderstandings between traditional project management offices (abbreviated in the following figure with PMO) and agile principles. In order to gather data, gain insights and then decide what to do, we used the method Same-and-Different (cf. Eoyang & Holladay, 2013, pos. 652-699 / p. 33-36). We implemented this method by using a table for collecting in a column labeled *same* - everything the two groups (PMO and agile principles) have in common. In another column labeled *different*, we gathered all the differentiators (see picture below).

We assembled all the data in the plenary. It was interesting how the group's spirit shifted when they realized that there are not only differences but also similarities between these two factions. As a matter of fact, for this group this was a great insight (it typically is when using this method for looking at different or even conflicting parties). We then took a closer look at the column entitled *different* for finding out which of these collected items really make a difference.

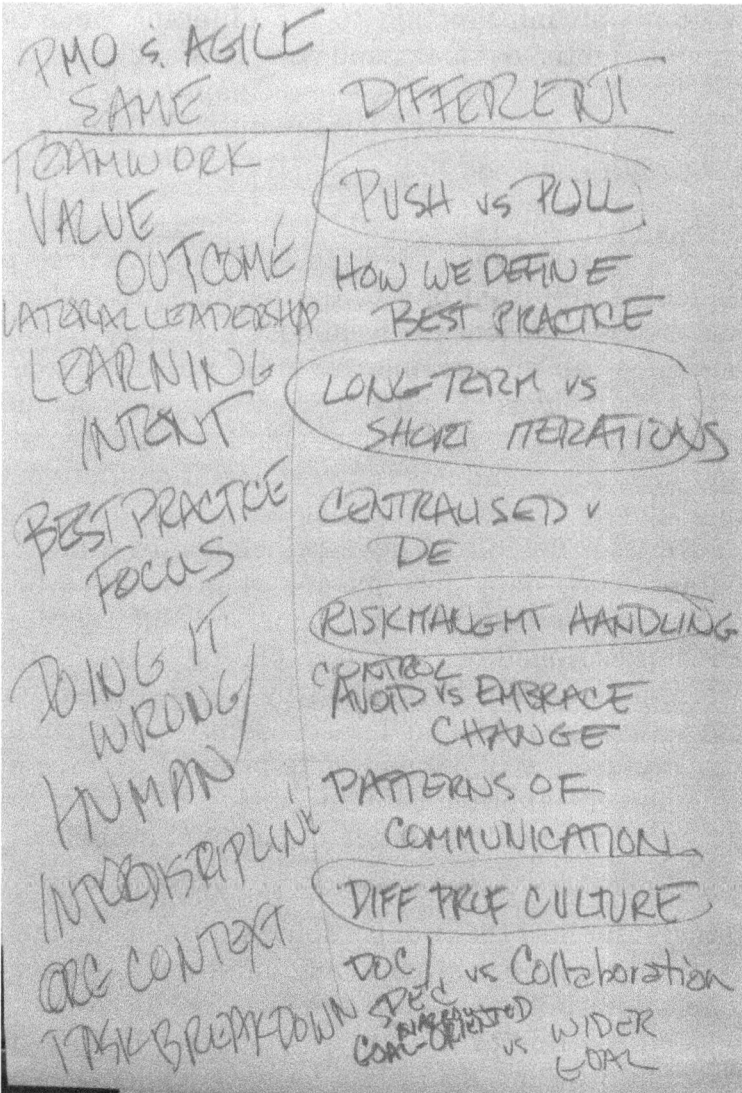

Same and Different (own illustration)

The next step would be to come up with actions for the things that make a difference, yet this was out of scope for this session. Therefore, our final step was to collect feedback on the applicability and usefulness of Retrospectives for Organizational Change yet as well on the session itself.

One of the participants reported that based on the Open Space session he attended at the RfG in 2012 (cf. Chapter 0) he already made good experiences using Retrospectives for Organizational Change while initializing and accompanying a change initiative in a software department. In his opinion such kind of retrospectives are particularly helpful in answering the question of "Why we want to change (now)?" when starting a change initiative. Using such retrospectives regularly during the change helps to decide whether the intended path supports the change or not. He emphasized that in his opinion change management in general, will benefit from Retrospectives for Organizational Change. Another participant pointed out that such kind of retrospectives bring a shared understanding of a context where everyone has different "parts of the puzzle." And moreover, that they support opportunities for the group to progress, improve their environment and build better relationships. However, he clarified that Retrospectives for Organizational Change are not the only way to initiate and implement change, but that they can certainly help.

8.2 Enabling Complex Change

As one example, a client –a multinational firm focusing on publishing and e-learning– struggled with their development processes for creating the e-learning software. I suggested conducting a Retrospective for Enabling Organizational Change to allow learning from experiences and uncover areas for change cf. Appendix. In this case, the goal was undefined – it was only described as "something needs to change". But neither what nor how was clear. The group of participants was composed of employees representing different areas of software development: project management, programmers, testers, business analysts, database experts, and software architects.

After setting the stage with a short introduction of all participants, clarifying the agenda, and the goal, we started gathering data by independently reflecting on individual experiences:

- What worked well? Should be done.
- What did hinder? Should be avoided.
- What was difficult? Should be watched out for.
- What was missing? Should be done.

Data was collected on sticky notes, using a color code for the four questions so that the differences between the recommendations and perspectives became visible. We were not looking for consensus but for different views. Therefore, we did not regard it as a problem if the same topic appeared on different colored sticky notes. We used those contradictions as a way to change our perspective. This is similar to what Graeßner explains as:

> „Experiences are suitable for indicating nuances of perceptions of a topic or evaluation of a problem." (Graeßner, 2008, p.109).

We collected these findings in the plenary and categorized them according to themes that emerged (cf. Stacey, 2011, p. 341). Moreover, we looked for patterns and surprises in the data collection. As a result of time constraints, the group prioritized the themes and concentrated only on the top four topics in the remaining time.

I asked them to split up in four subgroups, where each subgroup worked on one of the topics. In order to generate insights into the topics, concentration on the problem aspect was the first task. Thus, the subgroups defined the problem and discussed what makes it difficult to solve this problem. This way they uncovered underlying beliefs, assumptions, and norms that are hindering a solution. Next, I invited them to look at possible gains, for deciding if it is worth investing more time for coming up with a solution strategy. With these two steps I wanted to make certain not to concentrate on fixing the problem, but to ensure double-loop learning (cf. Argyris & Schön, 1978, p. 18-26). Then I asked them to decide what to do by defining actions for the problems.

Similar to the facilitation method World Café, between all of these steps –defining the problem, instigating in the possible gains and working on the solution strategies– each subgroup moved to a different topic, by leaving –with every switch an alternate-host behind (cf. Brown, 2005). The host served as a greeter and ensured that the new subgroup understood what has been discussed so far. For example, one group examined the problem space of the first topic, then moved on to the second topic for analyzing its possible gains and finally turned to the third topic in order to develop a solution strategy. This way everyone could contribute to all the different topics and moreover the quality of the outcome increased. This is one of the main advantages of World Café:

> „Small, intimate conversations link and build on each other as people move between groups, cross-pollinate ideas, and discover new insights into questions or issues that really matter [...]." (Brown, 2005, Pos. 284)

Additionally, this approach ensured that all participants took ownership of all results. In the original World Café subgroups are working on the same topic, whereas in this approach they were working on different ones (yet answering the same questions).

Finally, all results were presented in the plenary and the participants decided, which changes to implement right away and which need approval or more elaboration.

The major benefit from using a Retrospective for Enabling Organizational Change for the participants and for the organization later on was that there was not any resistance to the change initiative. The main reason was the involvement and the acknowledgment of the experiences of the participants, which was supported by having representatives of the different fields present.

8.3 Enabling Dynamic Change

In this application, my client –an agency designing and developing web-portals for their customers– wanted to switch from a traditional software development process to an agile one. The goal was clear yet the client did not know how to approach this goal and there was no direct path toward the goal. The organization wanted one particular project to start implementing this change. Everyone in this project participated in this Retrospective for Enabling Organizational Change cf. Appendix.

After general introductions, I started the session with a simulation, which allowed the group to experience an agile process. Then we discussed the value system and principles of the Agile Manifesto. This was all part of setting the stage. Then I asked the participants to individually brainstorm on the applicability of agile development within their environment by answering the following questions:

1. What is applied already?
2. What will be easy to be applied?
3. What will be difficult to apply?
4. What seems to be impossible?

The rationale for these questions was motivating the individuals to reflect on the situation – as it appeared in the past, how it is now and how it could be. With the first question, in addition to understanding what is already applied, I wanted to learn about possible misunderstandings of agile approaches. The second question focused on goals that are easy to reach (often colloquially called low-hanging-fruits) in contrast to the third question. With the last question I wanted to make the organization's culture more tangible. In some organizations when I ask this last question, the group comes up with a lot of things that seem to be impossible in the existing environment. In other organizations the attitude of the people is that generally everything is possible, and only some things will be hard to implement.

Similar to the previous example on enabling complex change, I asked individuals to present their findings. Then, we clustered these according to emerging topics. Next, I invited the participants to prioritize the topics, so that we could work on the top three. Again, I encouraged them to split into subgroups. Each subgroup worked on one topic and discussed what should be done and what should be avoided in the context of this topic. They then derived actions from this discussion that were presented to the whole group. This was the moment when the participants decided jointly on their commitment to implement some of the actions. Making these actions real was part of the transfer before we summarized the whole session in the closing.

Although some of the actions needed more discussion and elaboration, the Retrospective for Enabling Organizational Change created a strong commitment from the whole group to start using an agile process. The main reason was that the process was owned by the team and not mandated from outside the group. For example, it was not my lecturing in a training session on how agile software development works and therefore this is how they have to implement it. Instead I provided enough input, so they knew where they could start. Because agile software development is about collaboration, feedback, and continuous learning –this encourages participants to adapt and adjust while applying the approach. Of course, starting with a Retrospective for Enabling Organizational Change also emphasizes this fact.

9. Reflection on the Suggested Method

It is beyond a doubt
that all our knowledge that begins with experience.

– Immanuel Kant

Kicking off a change initiative using a Retrospective for Enabling Organizational Change is one thing. Another is, to implement and sustain the change. Holding regular Retrospectives for Organizational Change –from every two weeks to every three months– helps to ensure this. It allows treating change iteratively – where the result of the last retrospective initiates the next change (cf. Eoyang & Holladay, 2013, pos. 1183 / p. 61). As a consequence, change occurs as an iterative process of outcomes triggering the next cycle of action. Argyris and Schön clarify this as follows:

> "This means that the good dialectic is not a steady state free from conditions for error, but an open-ended process in which cycles of organizational learning create new conditions for error to which members of the organization respond by transforming

them so as to set in motion the next phase of inquiry." (Argyris & Schön, 1978, p. 144)

For successful change management a few other important parameters are needed (cf. Bunker & Alban, 2007, pos. 6531-6601):

- **Leadership involvement**: Leadership has to be authentic. Asking for everyone's perspective and then ignoring it does not support commitment. However, leadership is not limited to people who are in a leadership position by authority or who are having the necessary experience and resources (cf. Senge et.al., 2011, pos. 891). Leaders in a change are often powerless people who have an ability to influence others (cf. Manns & Rising, 2005, p. 6).
- **Capacity building**: This refers to creating the necessary capacity inside the organization. The skills for effectively using Retrospectives for Organizational Change have to be mastered within the organization. Real change, in terms of double-loop learning cannot happen if the group depends on a heroic rescuer (cf. Derby & Larsen, 2006, p. 148).
- **Credibility attainment**: Using small changes that make a big difference support gaining credibility. Starting with the toughest problem might take too long for sustaining the support for the change initiative. As Kotter points out:
  „The whole point is not to maximize short-term results at the expense of the future. The point is to make sure that visible results lend sufficient credibility to the transformation effort." (Kotter, 2012, pos. 1745-1754 / p. 128-129)

Although a Retrospective for Enabling Organizational Change is a powerful method for initiating and implementing a change, the success of a change project relies on the involvement of influencing leadership, on the capacity that is built within the group of people involved in the change, and on gaining credibility by implementing changes that have an impact.

10. Closing Remarks

Learning is like rowing against the current.
As soon as you stop,
you drift back.

– Benjamin Britten

Although originally designed for examining a fixed period of time and for reflecting on a shared history, retrospectives seem to be a way to initiating something new. What appears to be a problem at first sight becomes an asset – because not being limited by the inspection of a timeframe and the reflection of shared experiences opens up new opportunities. People are invited to bring their experiences from different projects and/or organizations so that learning can happen on a broader scale. Especially if the group involved in a dynamic or complex change has nothing in common so far, they will benefit from the diversity of their individual experiences. Natalie Knapp emphasizes that nobody has the possibility to capture all the different facets of what is happening (cf. Knapp, 2013, pos. 619) and furthermore:

> „Everything indicates that we can do justice to the complexity of the world only

by developing solutions jointly: Self-orga-
nizing processes have to interweave dif-
ferent cultures, abilities, and attitudes to
new ideas, that satisfy the diverse needs."
(Knapp, 2013, pos. 3272-3274)

Certainly, Retrospectives for Organizational Change
are not the only instruments for change management, there are many resources pointing to other
helpful methods (cf. for example Holman, Devane &
Cady, 2007 or Bunker & Alban, 2007). The strength
however, lies in leveraging individual experiences.
Using experiences to enable change requires seeing
the past from a different perspective. Stacey makes
this point:

"[...] we know the past through the present.
[...] the hypotheses we form about the past,
depend upon the viewpoint of the present,
which will change in the future. In other
words, the future will change the meaning
of the past." (Stacey, 2011, p. 319)

Knapp emphasizes that the awareness we create in
the present about the past can create a two-way
coupling by influencing both the past and the future
(cf. Knapp, 2013, pos. 1261-1262). Yet, analyzing
past experience means more than gathering data. It
requires everyone involved to reflect on the past as
it is individually understood right now. This relates
to the experience of one of the early adopters of
Retrospectives for Organizational Change (cf. Chapter 7.1). He stressed that such a retrospective help
the people involved understand the purpose of the

change. This understanding creates the necessary commitment. Additionally, at both RfG conferences all professional retrospective facilitators emphasized the usefulness of Retrospectives for Organizational Change.

Nowadays, organizations face many different challenges that are interdependent and often marked by high uncertainty and unpredictability. Using individuals' different perspectives helps to understand better what is implied by such kind of change. Retrospectives for Organizational Change help address these challenges – not only for initiating the change but for learning more about it during the implementation. Implementing feedback cycles –e.g. with retrospectives– is the recommended strategy for ensuring learning while implementing the change (cf. Beckhard & Pritchard, 1992, p. 9). Because:

"Learning and change processes are part of each other. Change is a learning process and learning is a change process." (ibid., p. 14)

Retrospectives for Organizational Change might trigger this learning process. However, living through it might need a different kind of support for the individual. Offering accompanying coaching for individuals as well as for the group might be required to overcome the challenges learning and change provides.

Reference List

Argyris, C. and Schön, D.A. (1978): *Organizational Learning: A Theory of Action Perspective*. Reading, Mass: Addison-Wesley Publishing Company.

Bandler, R. and Grinder, J. (1975): *Patterns of the Hypnotic Techniques of Milton H. Erickson*, M.D. Volume 1. Cupertino, CA: Grinder & Associates.

Beckhard, R. and Pritchard, W. (1992): *Changing the Essence: The Art of Creating and Leading Fundamental Change in Organizations*. San Francisco, CA: Jossey-Bass.

Bogsnes, B. (2008, ebook): *Implementing Beyond Budgeting. Unlocking the Performance Potential*. Hoboken, NJ: Wiley. Kindle ed.

Brown, J. (2005): *The World Café: Shaping our Futures through Conversations that matter*. San Francisco, CA: Berrett-Koehler Publishers, Kindle ed.

Bunker, B.B. and Alban, B.T. (2007, ebook): *The Handbook of Large Group Methods: Creating Systemic Change in Organizations and Communities*. San Francisco, CA: Jossey-Bass. Kindle ed.

Eckstein, J. (2004): *Agile Software Development in the Large: Diving into the Deep*. New York, NY: Dorset House Publishing.

Eckstein, J. (2010): *Agile Software Development with Distributed Teams: Staying Agile in a Global World*. New York, NY: Dorset House Publishing.

Eoyang, G. (2009): *Coping with Chaos: Seven Simple Tools*. Circle Pines, MN: Lagumo.

Eoyang, G. and Holladay, R. (2013, ebook): *Adaptive Action: Leveraging Uncertainty in Your Organization*. Stanford, CA: Stanford University Press. Kindle ed.

Derby, E. and Larsen, D. (2006): *Agile Retrospectives. Making Good Teams Great*. Raleigh, NC: Pragmatic Bookshelf.

Gladwell, M. (2000): *The Tipping Point. How Little Things Can Make a Big Difference*. New York, NY: Back Bay Books/Little, Brown and Company.

Gleick, J. (2011, ebook): *Chaos – Making a new Science*. New York, NY: Open Road Media Iconic Ebooks, Kindle ed.

Graeßner, G. (2008): *Moderation – das Lehrbuch*. Augsburg: ZIEL Verlag.

Gratton, L. (2011, ebook): *The Shift. The future of work is already here*. London, UK: Harper Collins Publishers Ltd., Kindle ed.

Gribbin, J. (2004, ebook): *Deep Simplicity. Chaos, Complexity and the Emergence of Life*. London, UK: Penguin Books Ltd., Kindle ed.

Holladay, R. and Quade, K. (2008): *Influencing Patterns for Change*. CreateSpace Independent Publishing Platform.

Holman, P., Devane, T., and Cady, S. (eds.) (2007): *The Change Handbook. The Definitive Resource on Today's Best Methods for Engaging Whole Systems.* San Francisco, CA: Berrett-Koehler Publishers Inc.

Karten, N. (2009): *Changing How You Manage and Communicate Change. Focusing on the human side of change.* Cambridgeshire, UK: IT Governance Publishing.

Kerth, N. (2001): *Project Retrospectives. A Handbook for Team Reviews.* New York, NY: Dorset House Publishing.

Knapp, N. (2013, ebook): *Kompass neues Denken: Wie wir uns in einer unübersichtlichen Welt orientieren können.* Reinbek bei Hamburg: Rowohlt Verlag, Kindle ed.

Kotter, J. (2012, ebook): *Leading Change.* Boston, Mass.: Harvard Business Review Press, Kindle ed.

Kurtz, C.F. and Snowden, D. (2003): *The new dynamics of strategy: Sense-making in a complex and complicated world* In: IBM Systems Journal, Vol.42, No.3, p.462-483. Available also online: http://tinyurl.com/kurtz-pdf[1]. Last accessed on March 22nd, 2013

Kua, P. (2013): *The Retrospective Handbook. A Guide for Agile Teams.* CreateSpace Independent Publishing Platform.

Lewin, K. (1947): *Frontiers in Group Dynamics: Concept, Method and Reality in Social Science; Social Equilibria and Social Change.* In: Human Relations

[1] http://tinyurl.com/kurtz-pdf

I. p. 5-41. http://hum.sagepub.com/content/1/1/5[2].
Last accessed March 27th, 2013

Manns, M.L. and Rising, L. (2005): *Fearless Change: Patterns for Introducing New Ideas*. Boston, MA: Pearson Education Inc.

Revans, R. (2011): *ABC of Action Learning*. Burlington, VT: Gower Publishing Company.

Rifkin, J. (2011): *Die dritte industrielle Revolution. Die Zukunft der –Wirtschaft nach dem Atomzeitalter*. Frankfurt: Campus Verlag.

Satir, V. et.al. (1991): *The Satir Model: Family Therapy and Beyond*. Palo Alto, CA: Science and Behavior Books Inc.

Scharmer, C.O. (2009, ebook): *Theory U: Learning from the Future as It Emerges*. San Francisco, CA: Berrett-Koehler Publishers, Kindle ed.

Seddon, J. (2003): *Freedom from Command and Control: A Better Way to Make the Work Work*. Buckingham, UK: Vanguard Consulting Ltd.

Seifert, J.W. (2011, ebook): *30 Minuten Modererieren*. Offenbach: Gabal Verlag, Kindle ed.

Senge, P. et.al. (1999): *The Dance of Change. The Challenges of Sustaining Momentum in Learning Organizations*. London, UK: Nicholas Brealey Publishing.

Senge, P. et.al. (2011, ebook): *The Necessary Revolution: How Individuals and Organisations Are Working Together to Create a Sustainable World*. Clerken-

---

[2] http://hum.sagepub.com/content/1/1/5

well, London, UK: Nicholas Brealey Publishing, Kindle ed.

Stacey, R.D. (1996): *Strategic Management and Organizational Dynamics*. London, UK: Pitman Publishing, 2nd ed.

Stacey, R.D. (2011): *Strategic Management and Organizational Dynamics*. Harlow, UK: Pearson Education Ltd., 6th ed.

Whitmore, J. (1996): *Coaching for Performance*. London, Sonoma: Nicholas Brealey Publishing, 2nd ed.

Zimmerman, B., Lindberg, C., and Plsek, P. (2008): *edgeware: lessons from complexity science for health care leaders*. V H A Incorporated (Curt Lindberg, Plexus Institute).

Appendix

Results from Open Space at RfG 2012/13

Photo protocol of the RfG 2012 – Open Space Session: Retrospectives as Tools for Change Management

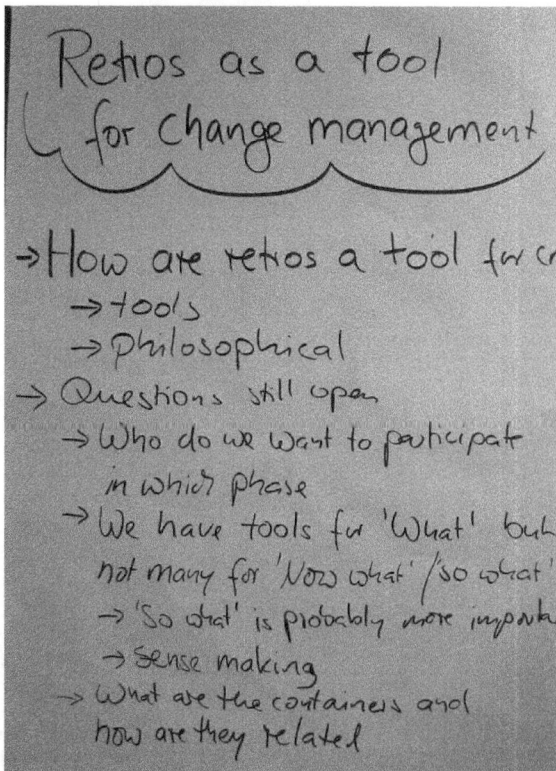

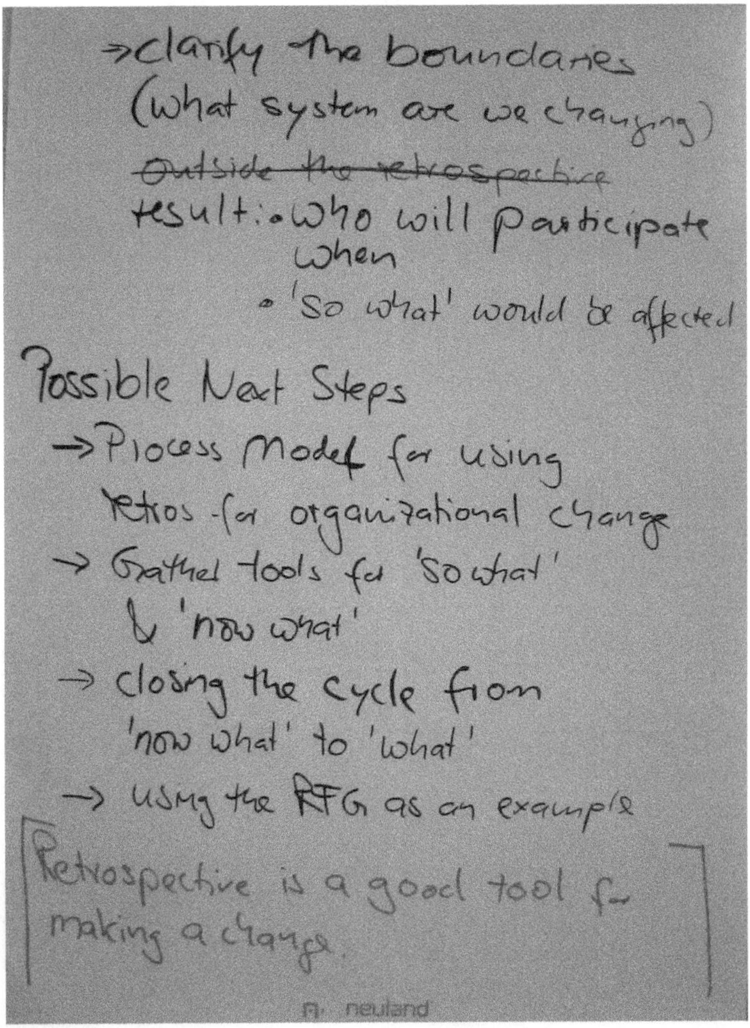

⇒ clarify the boundaries
(what system are we changing)

~~Outside the retrospective~~

result: ○ who will participate
when
○ 'So what' would be affected

Possible Next Steps

→ Process Model for using
retros for organizational change
→ Gather tools for 'So what'
& 'now what'
→ closing the cycle from
'now what' to 'what'
→ using the RFG as an example

Retrospective is a good tool for
making a change.

A. neuland

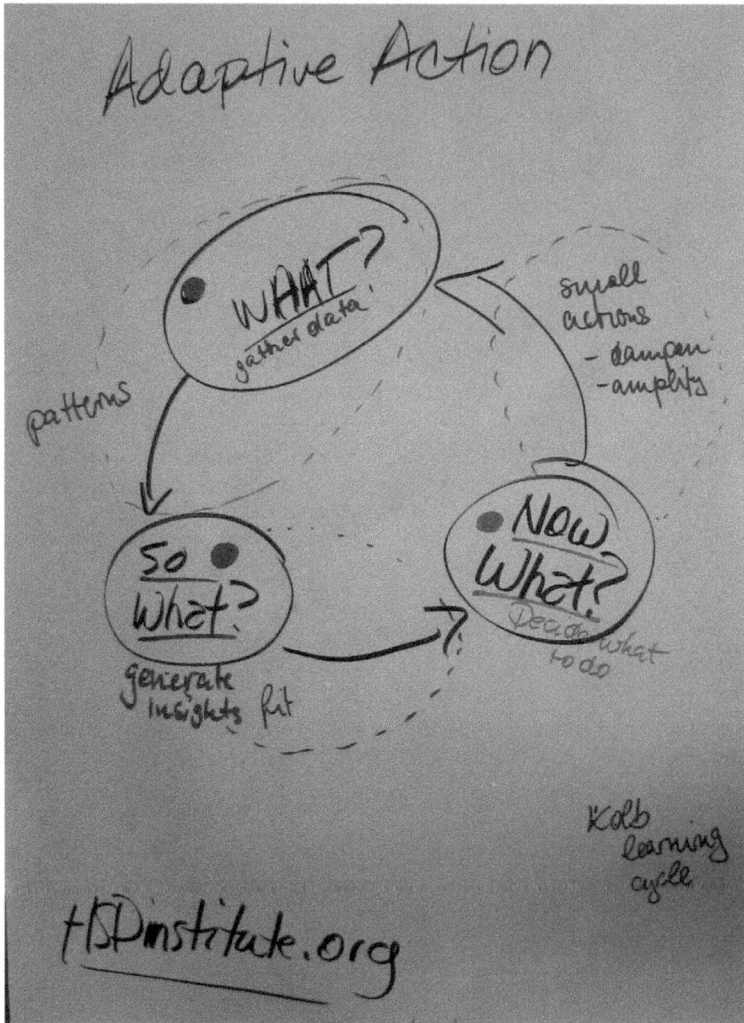

Adaptive Action

WHAT?
gather data

So
What?
generate
insights fit

NOW
What?
Decide what
to do

patterns

small
actions
- dampen
- amplify

Kolb
learning
cycle

HSDinstitute.org

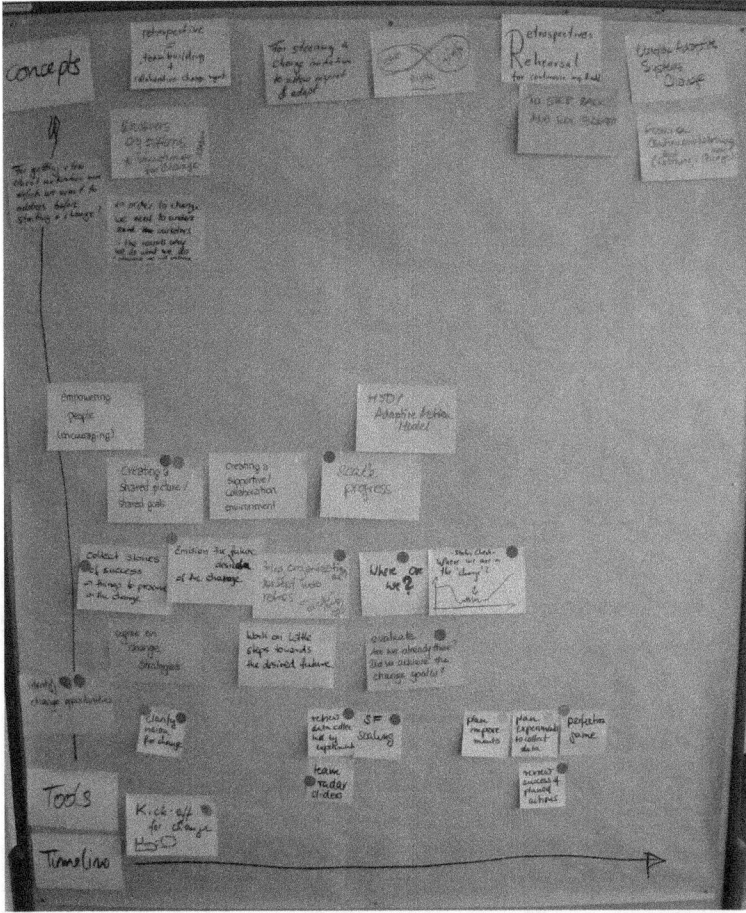

Photo protocol of the RfG 2012 – Open Space Session: Retrospectives for Organizational Change

Works	does not work
→ Community meetings → CoPs	→ data bases → management of facilitators
→ Open Space days of /for experience exchange	→ small group consoli- dating retro data
→ connecting people	↓ distribution of the data
→ data base + social network + semantic search	emails newsletters
→ connectors, e.g. managers, facilitators "living sign posts"	
→ knowledge broker: facilitator experts CoPs using patterns e.g. in the retro kick-off	
→ Retro as kick-off for projects	would help but not without people

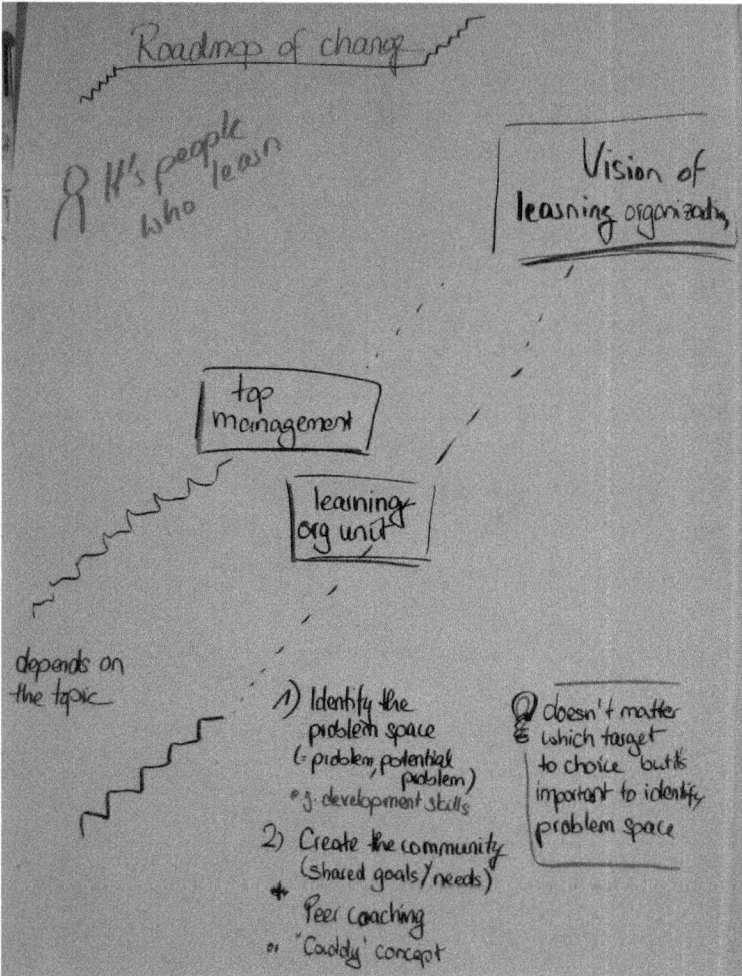

What?
So What?
Now What?
Collective Drawing
Wear s/o else's hat
de Bono's Thinking Hats
In another company,
Myths, Legends, Monsters
Magic Wand

Photo protocol of the RfG 2013 – Open Space Session: Retrospectives for Organizational Change

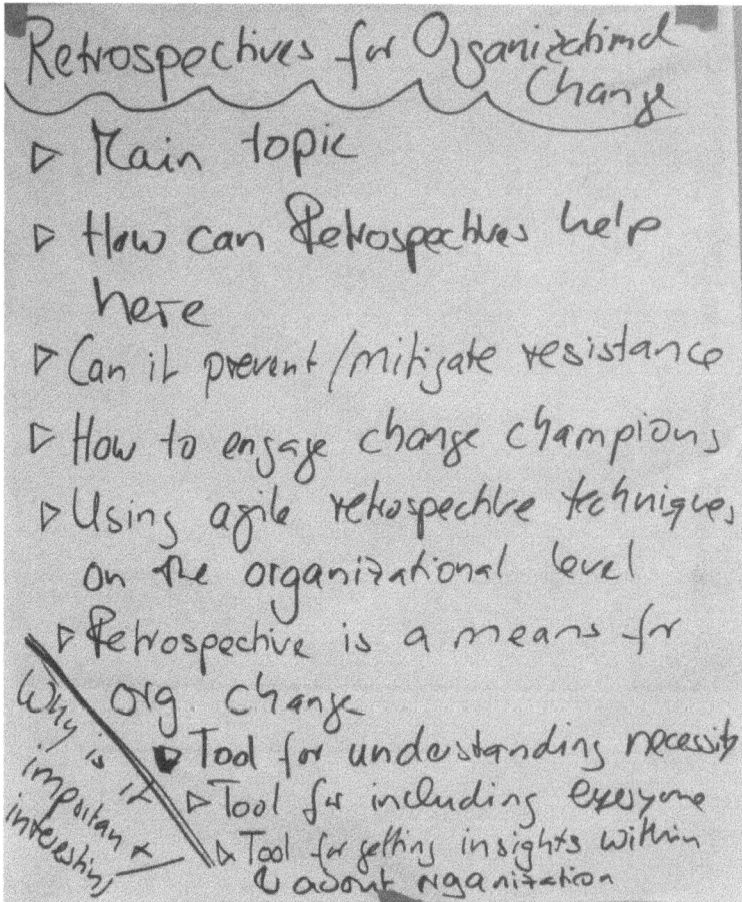

Retrospectives for Organizational Change

▷ Main topic

▷ How can Retrospectives help here

▷ Can it prevent/mitigate resistance

▷ How to engage change champions

▷ Using agile retrospective techniques on the organizational level

▷ Retrospective is a means for org. change

Why is it important & interesting?

▷ Tool for understanding necessity
▷ Tool for including everyone
▷ Tool for getting insights within & about organization

Tools / Tips

→ Radar Diagrams: anonimously collect
   data on what you want to measure
→ What do you want to ~~do to~~ achieve/avoid
   (Coaching Model)
→ Minimum 3h
→ Use some kind of timeline
→ continuous timeline (colourcoding)
→ Switching/Pairing → elaborating different perspectives

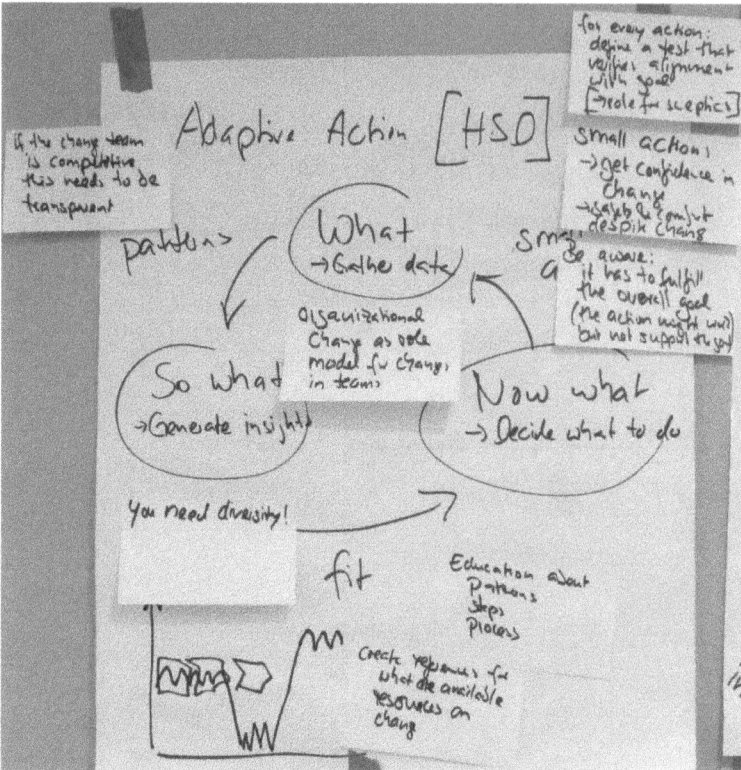

Protocol of Workshop at XP 2013

Retrospectives as a Tool for Change Management

Handout enriched with pictures from the session XP 2013, Vienna, May 6th, 2013. Session conducted by Jutta Eckstein & Diana Larsen

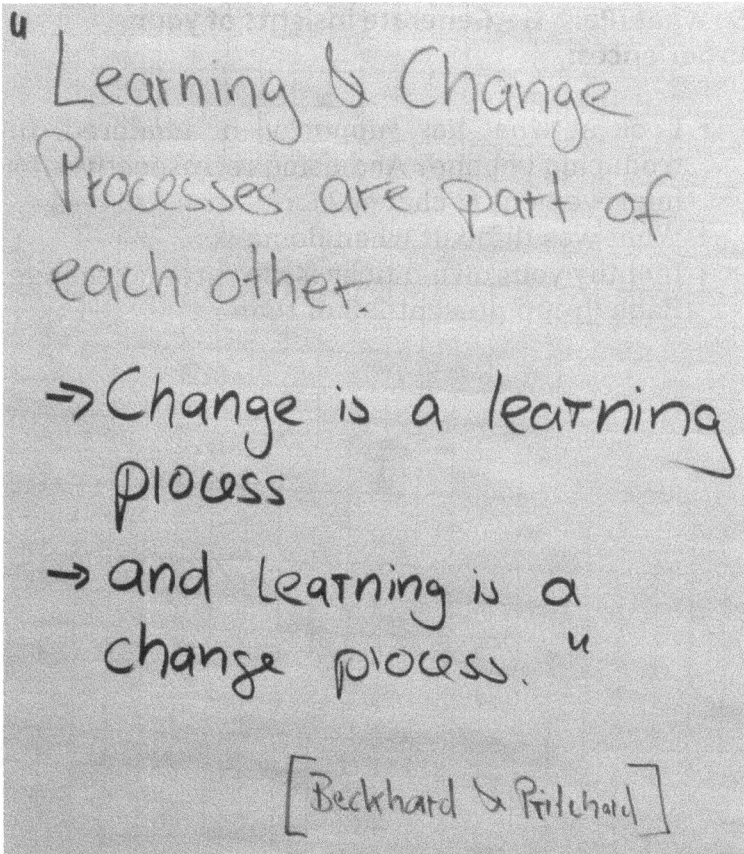

Learning & Change Processes are part of each other.

→ Change is a learning process

→ and learning is a change process. "

[Beckhard & Pritchard]

Welcoming flipchart for setting the stage

Brief Introduction to Set the Stage

What – Your experience in:

- Introducing desired change?
- Using retrospectives for sparking continuous improvement & instigating beneficial process change for teams/organizations?

So what (Part 1) – Generate insights of your experiences:

- Look at what has supported or hindered: Introducing change? And using retrospectives for improvement & change?
- What was difficult when doing so.
- Identify your own "sticky issue" around change. Each group present 2-3 of them.

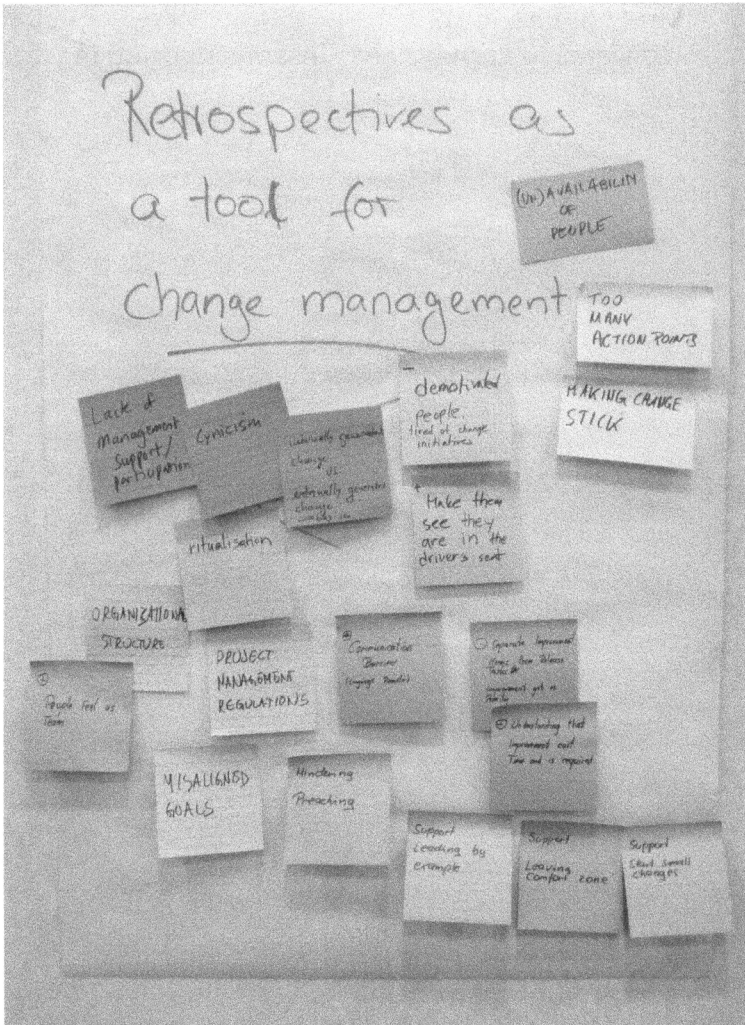

Collection of stickie issues

So what (Part 2) – digging deeper into your topic

- What are the new possibilities for managing change (e.g. like Adaptive Action, or different

kinds of change)?
- How can you apply these lessons learned in your context?

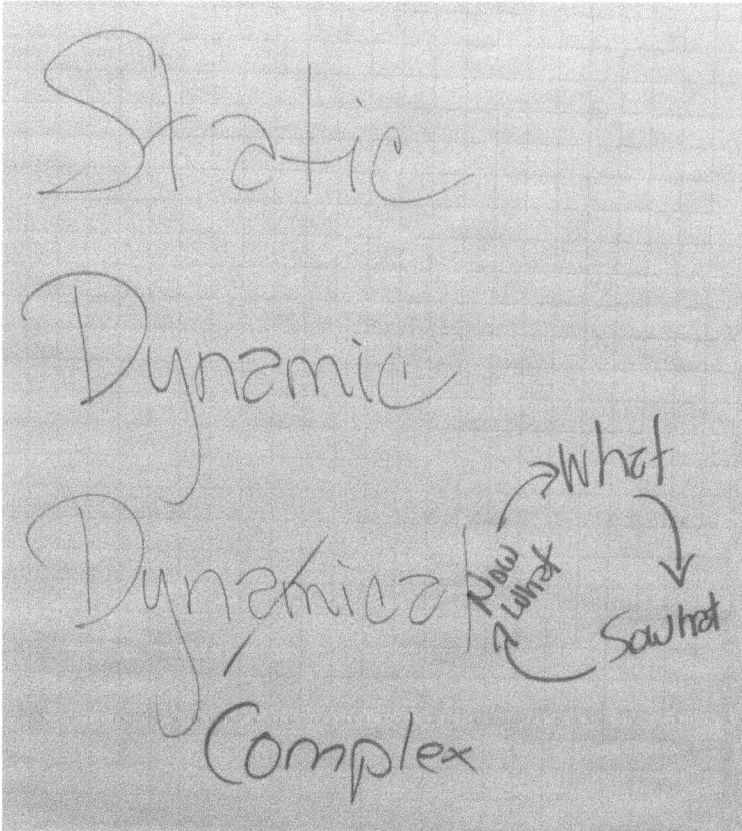

Introduction of: 3 kinds of change and adaptive action

Now what/Decide what to do:

- How can we shape retrospective so these meetings can support desired change?

- How can you apply the methods, tools, and lessons learned to your impediments to change and "sticky issues"?
- How can we leverage the methods, tools, and lessons learned to overcome these obstacles?

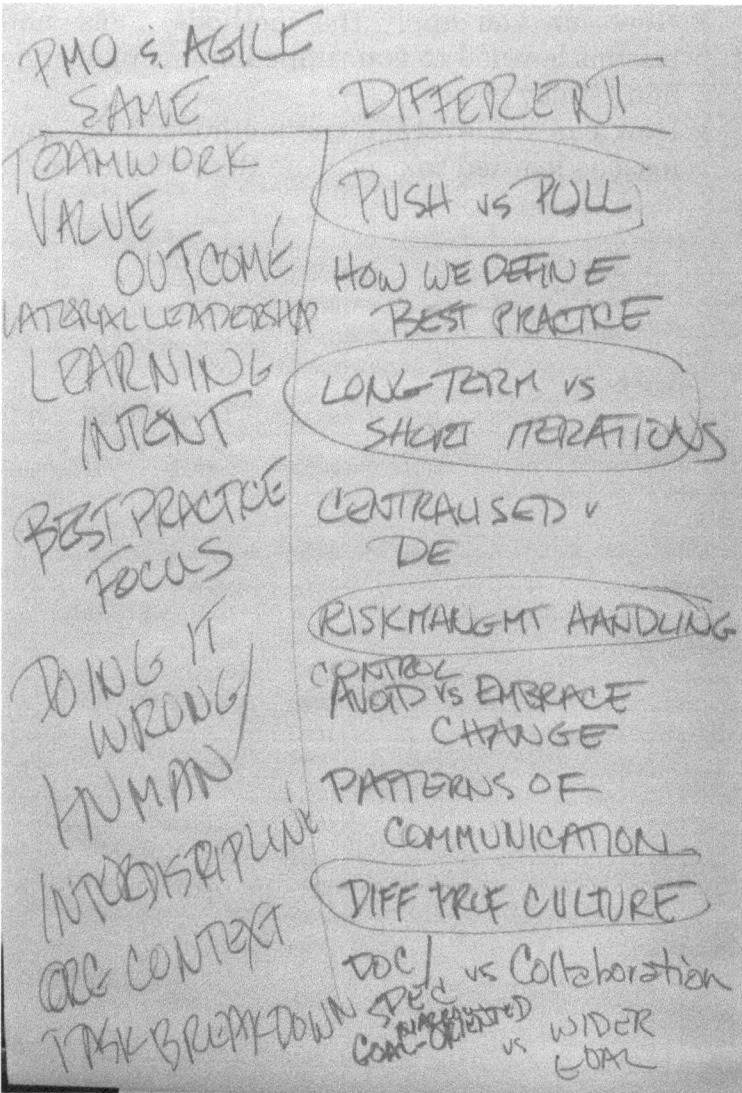

Same & Different for the stickie issue: Project Management Regulations (which often hinder agility)

Closing

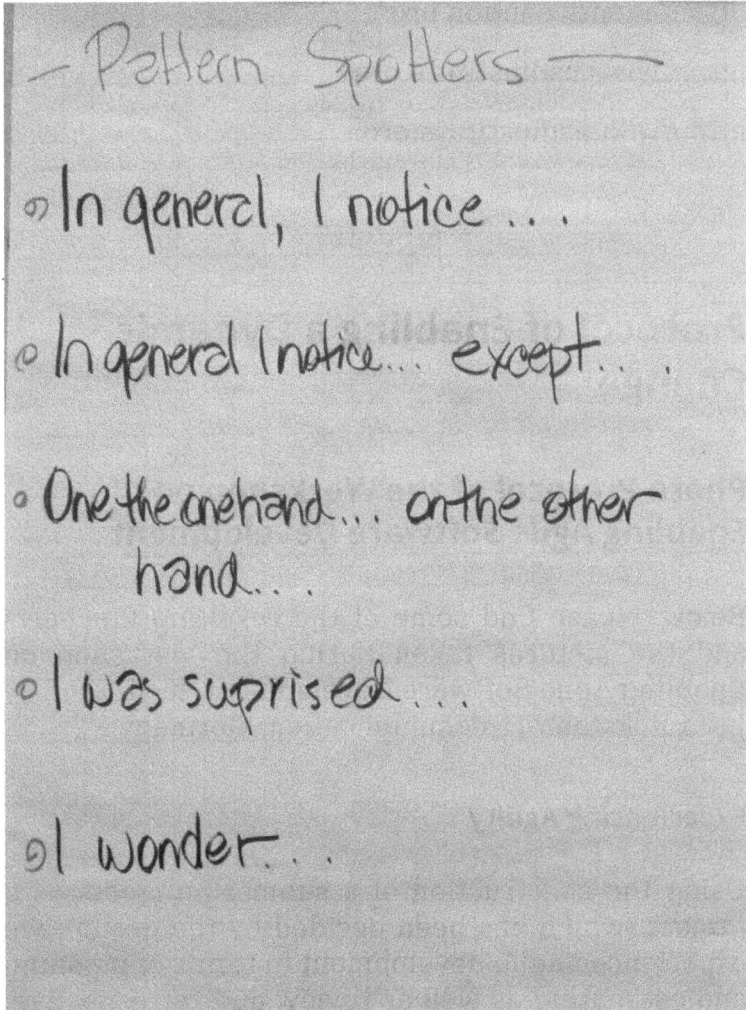

- Pattern Spotters -

- In general, I notice ...

- In general I notice ... except ...

- One the one hand ... on the other hand ...

- I was suprised ...

- I wonder ...

We used so-called pattern spotters for obtaining feedback (and for offering one more tool)

Useful URLs

http://adaptiveaction.org[3]

http://www.hsdinstitute.org[4]

http://wiki.hsdinstitute.org[5]

Protocol of Enabling a Dynamic Change

Photo Protocol of the Workshop on Enabling Agile Software Development

Below, please find some of the resulting flipcharts and the pictures taken during the workshop on Enabling Agile Software Development, facilitated by Jutta Eckstein, IT communication, Germany.

Experiencing Agility

Using the construction of a submarine model as a project (which has been decided by the group), we experienced agile development in terms of planning and estimating as well as review and retrospective. For doing so, we split up into two teams.

---

[3] http://adaptiveaction.org
[4] http://www.hsdinstitute.org
[5] http://wiki.hsdinstitute.org

Estimating and Planning in Iterations

The product owners presented the prioritized features to their teams. We used planning poker for estimating the features. Based on the estimates and the priorities we came up with an iteration plan. For each iteration we had ten minutes in order to construct the submarine model.

Iteration Review and Retrospective

For the review, the team presented their accomplishments; the product owner reviewed the outcome and decided on acceptance or rejection of the delivered features..

In the retrospectives we reflected on things that worked well and things that should be improved. We then decided on 1-3 things we want to do differently in the next ten-minute-iteration in order to being more effective.

Well ☺ | Needs improvement ☹

± Work assignment   more client interaction
good solutions   thinking ahead / integration
                           which features are built
                           work assignment (specs)

Difficult ?   Actions:

                           - more client contact
                           - assign client represented
                           - better initial planning

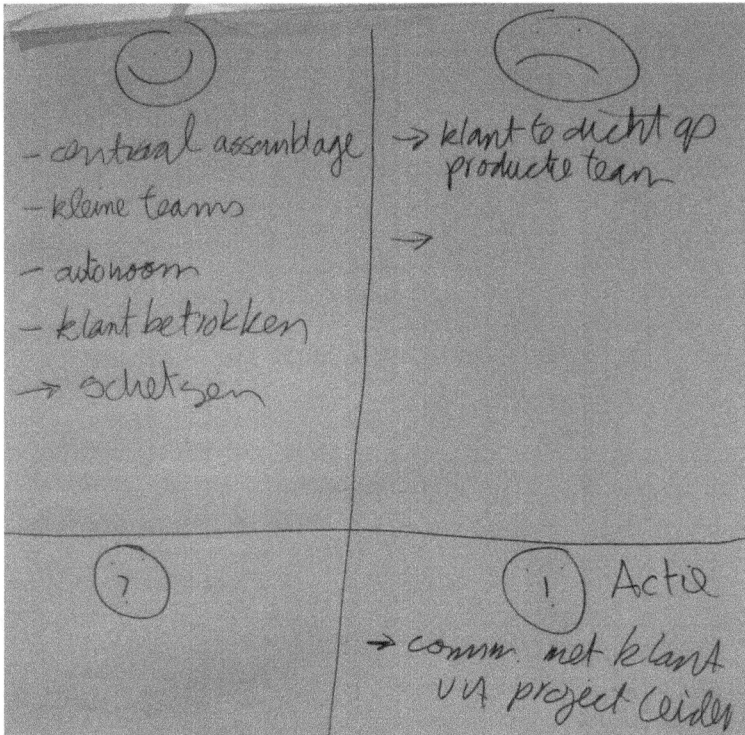

Release

Below are the final submarine models created by the two different teams over two ten-minute- iterations.

Applicability of Agility

This part of the workshop was preceded by a discussion on the both the value system and the principles of the Agile Manifesto with the goal of conveying a solid knowledge and theoretical background on agility.

Next we brainstormed individually on the applicability of agility in our own project environment and used a color code to illustrate what we think will be easy and what will be difficult to implement. Thereafter, we clustered the result of this brainstorming into subject areas.

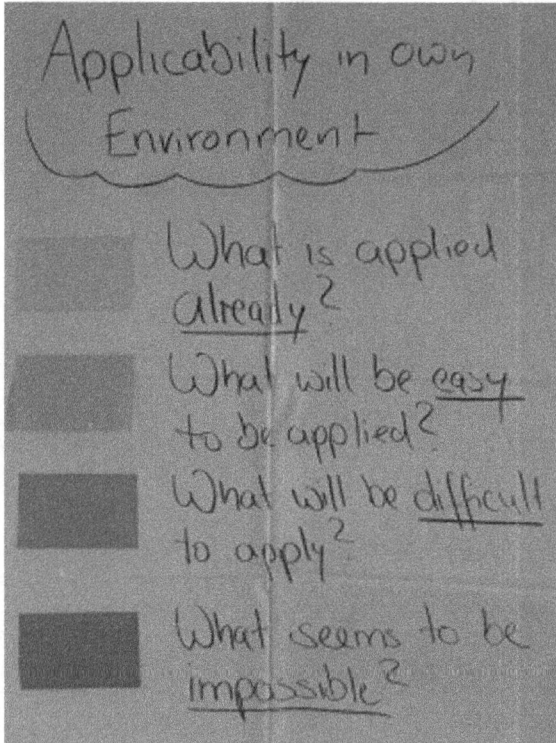

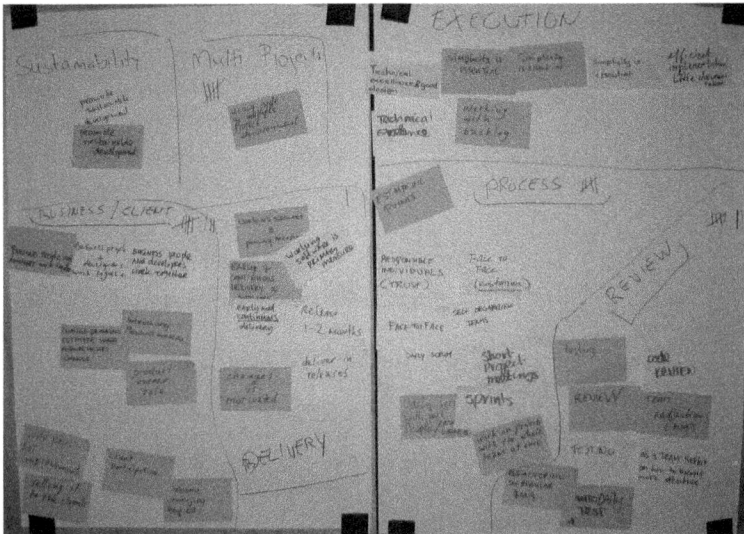

Then we prioritized these subject areas for figuring out what we want to focus on in the remaining time. The following list includes our top 3:

- Business / client
- Process
- Review

Coming up with a Solution Strategy

We split up in three groups. Each group worked on one of these highest prioritized subjects. We concentrated on finding out the following specifics for each topic:

- What should be done?
- What should be avoided?

While presenting the outcome the team decided to put some of the strategies into action, which are stated separately in this document.

However, during this presentation it became clear that for several issues a more detailed discussion will be needed in order to decide on concrete actions. The whole team will have to decide to what extent the discussed suggestions will come into real.

Business / Client

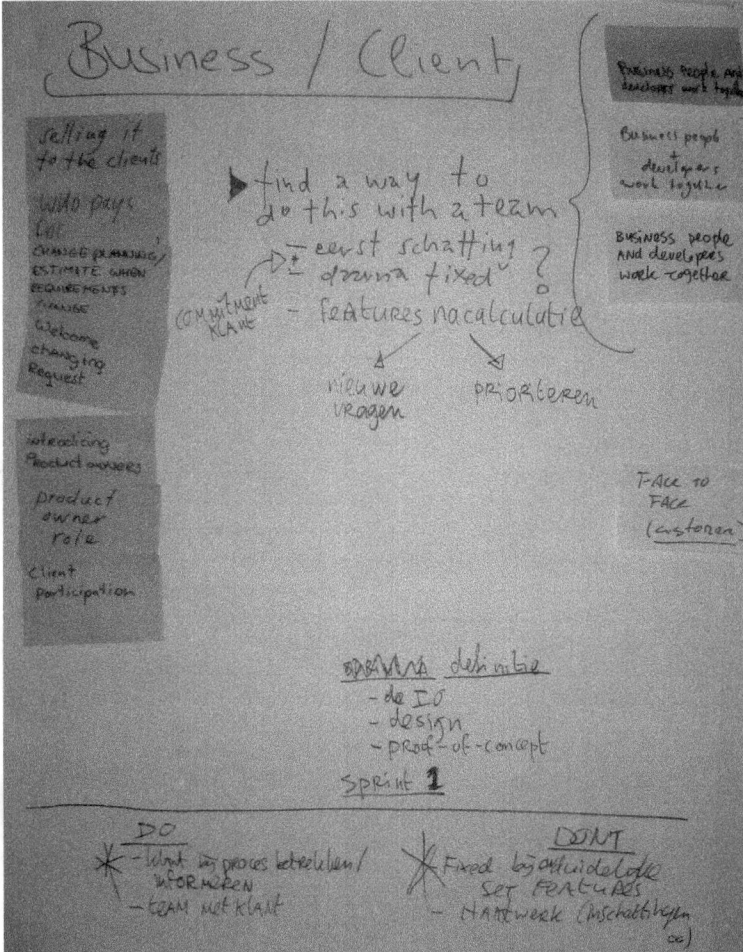

In terms of business / client the team agreed to put the following into reality:

- Don't accept / offer fixed price for a set of features

• Involve the client in the process

Process

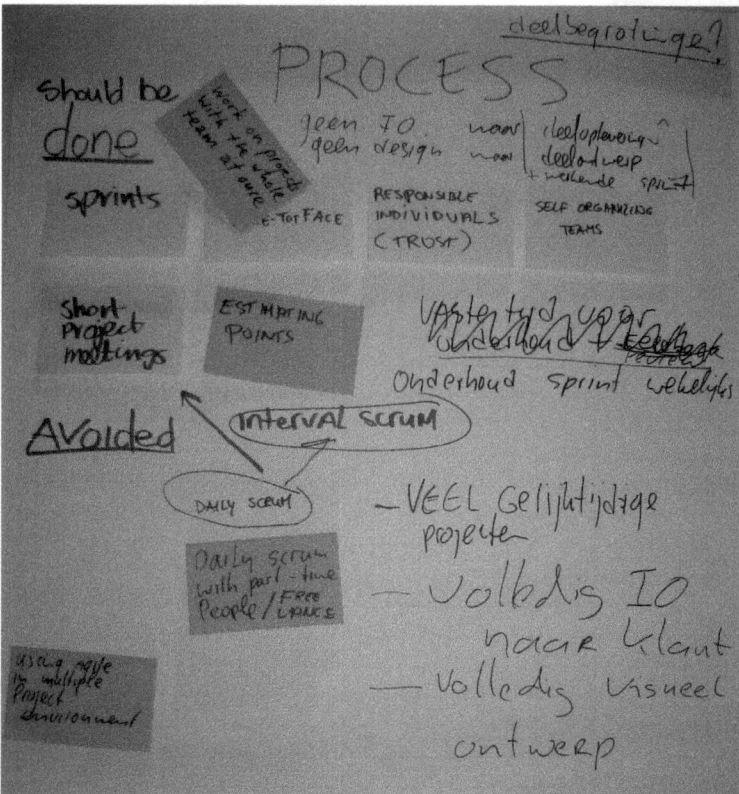

In terms of the process, the team decided to implement the following:

• Daily Scrum

Review

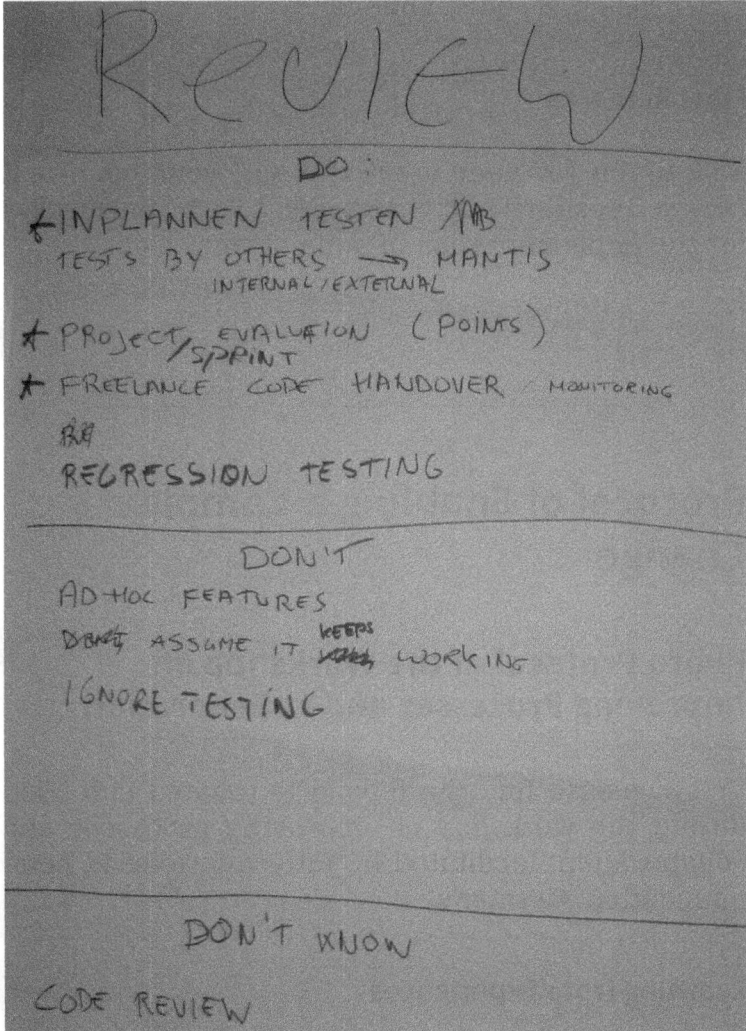

In terms of review, the team decided on putting the following strategies into real:

- Plan for testing
- Project and sprint evaluation
- Freelance code handover

Final Remarks

Thank you for your creativity and your open and honest questions and comments. I wish you success for the implementation of agile development!

Jutta Eckstein

Protocol of Enabling a Complex Change

Photo Protocol of the Workshop on Improving Processes and Collaboration

Below, please find the flipcharts created and used during the workshop on improving processes and collaboration, facilitated by Jutta Eckstein, IT communication, Germany.

Learning from Experiences

After setting the stage by clarifying for example the goal for the workshop, we brainstormed individually on our past experiences and used a color code to illustrate what has helped and what has hindered us in the past. Next we clustered the result of this brainstorming into subject areas.

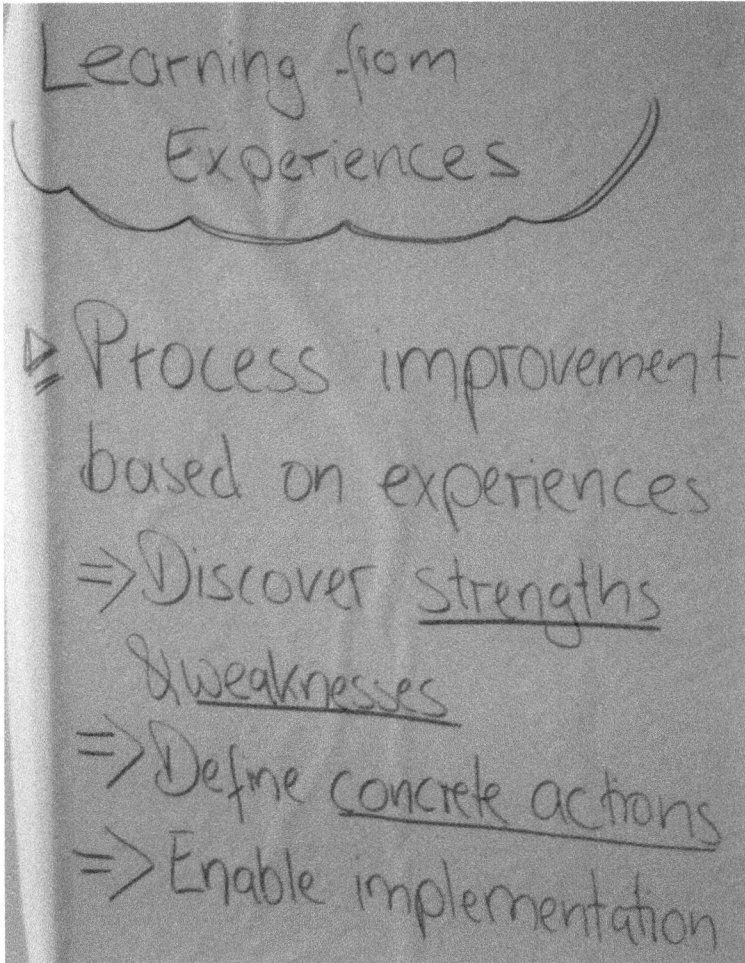

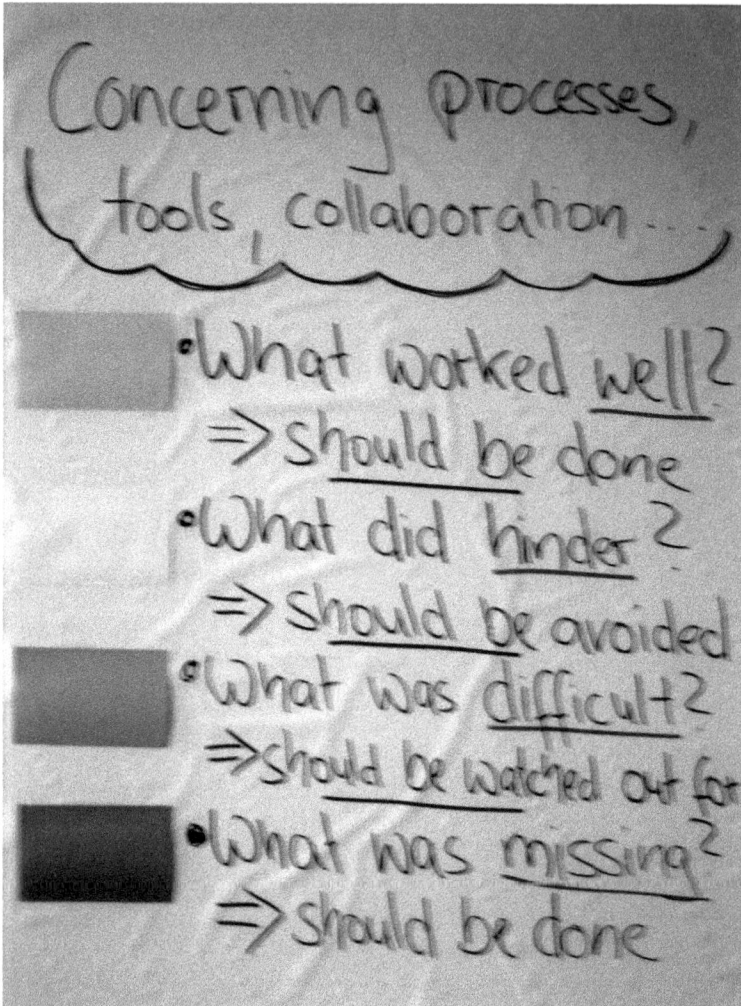

Concerning processes, tools, collaboration...

- What worked well?
  ⇒ should be done
- What did hinder?
  ⇒ should be avoided
- What was difficult?
  ⇒ should be watched out for
- What was missing?
  ⇒ should be done

Then we prioritized these subject areas for figuring out what we want to focus on in the remaining time. Each participant had three marks for voting on his or her most important topic. The following topics emerged as the most significant ones:

- Planning
- Vision
- Product Owner
- Capturing Requirements

I recommend to come back and examine the remaining topics at another point in time.

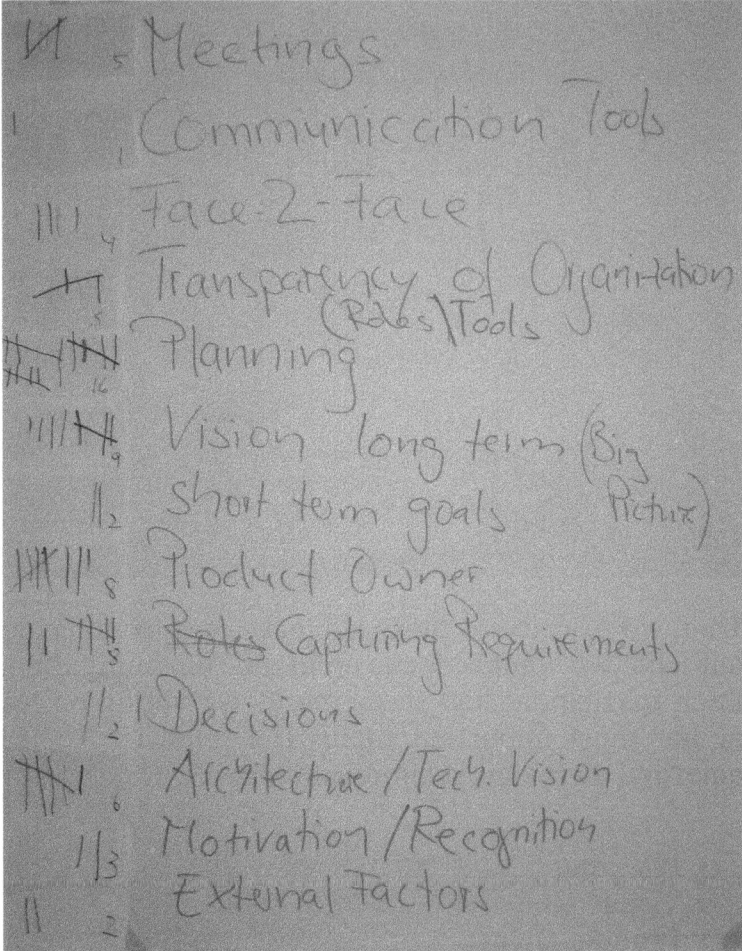

VI   Meetings
I   Communication Tools
III   Face-2-Face
VII   Transparency of Organization (Roles/Tools)
TTT TTT   Planning
IIITTT   Vision long term (Big Picture)
II   Short term goals
TTTII   Product Owner
II TTT   Roles Capturing Requirements
II   Decisions
TTTI   Architecture / Tech. Vision
II   Motivation / Recognition
II   External Factors

Action Planning

We split up in four groups. Each group worked in turns on three of the four highest prioritized subjects. After working on one of the guiding questions, we switched to the next topic and worked on this answering the next question. We used the following questions as a guidance for our conversations:

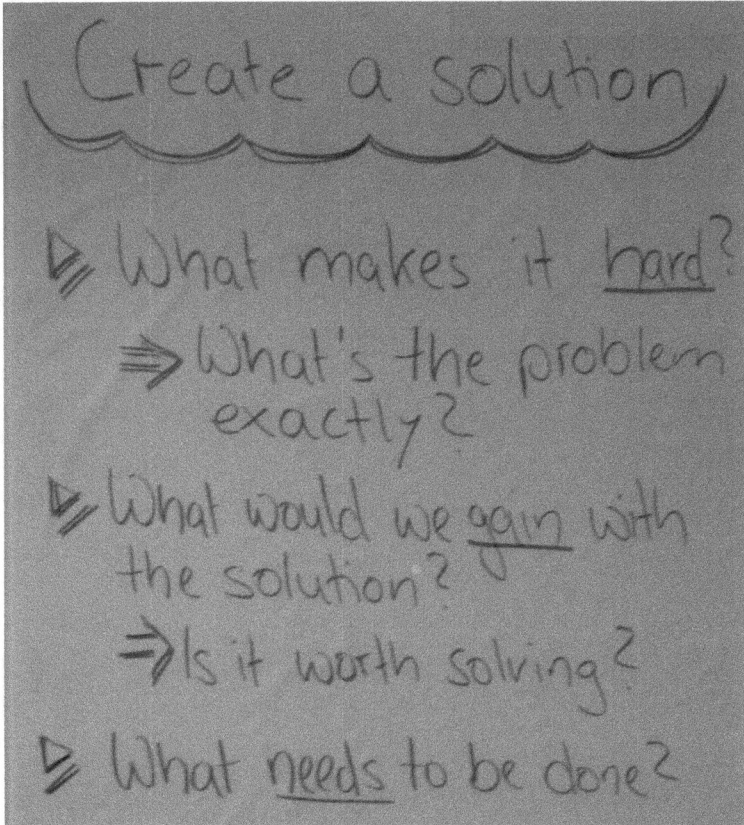

Create a solution

▷ What makes it <u>hard</u>?
⇒ What's the problem exactly?
▷ What would we <u>gain</u> with the solution?
⇒ Is it worth solving?
▷ What <u>needs</u> to be done?

For answering the last question we tried to come up with concrete actions. In the plenary we presented the discussion results for all topics. We tried to come up with a commitment to what we want to do differently in the near future. For some areas we could even commit to concrete actions for other areas we could only agree to the necessary change but not to concrete actions for the change. The reason was that the latter topics depend on other decisions e.g. by the steering committee.

Capture Requirements

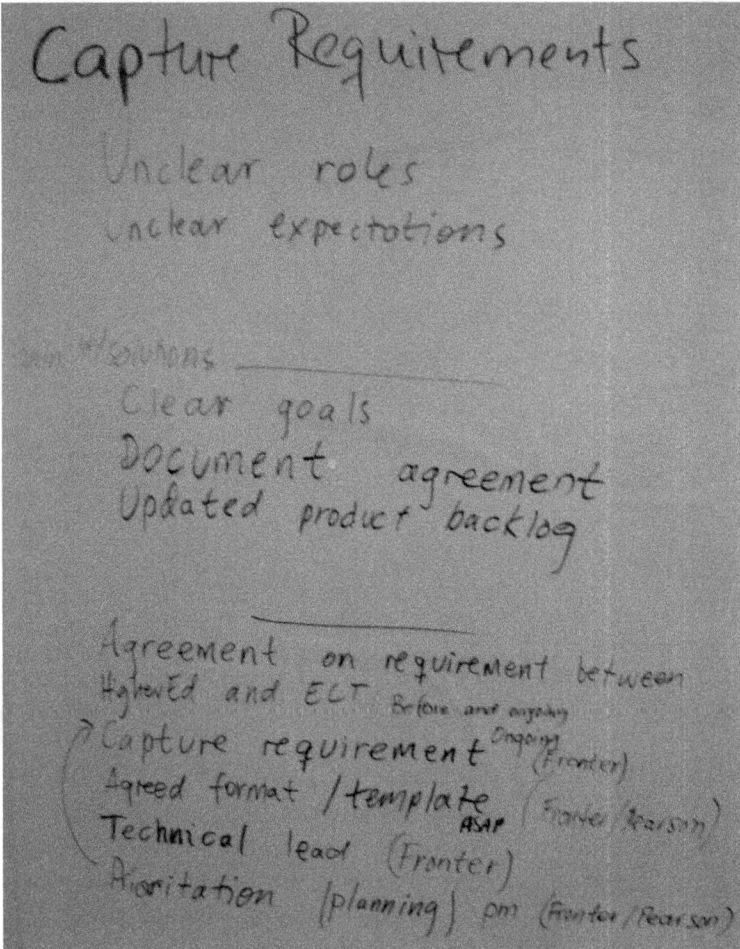

There was the commitment by the team to agree on a format template in the next few days.

Product Owner

Product Owner

What makes it hard? - Lack of definition
- Multiple product owners
- Who ~~comes~~ makes final decision
- no well defined scope - possibility of conflicting scope
- 100% dedicated? No

Solution - 1| HE
| Frontier
| ELT

1 Decision maker - AI to be done by Steering Cte at next meeting

2. Agreed upon definition of Prod. Owner role + time commitment
AI to be done at next meeting

Note: Role time commitment is 100% for the at least through 2012

The team decided to bring these suggestions to the attention of the steering committee, because the team can’t make a commitment on this level.

Vision

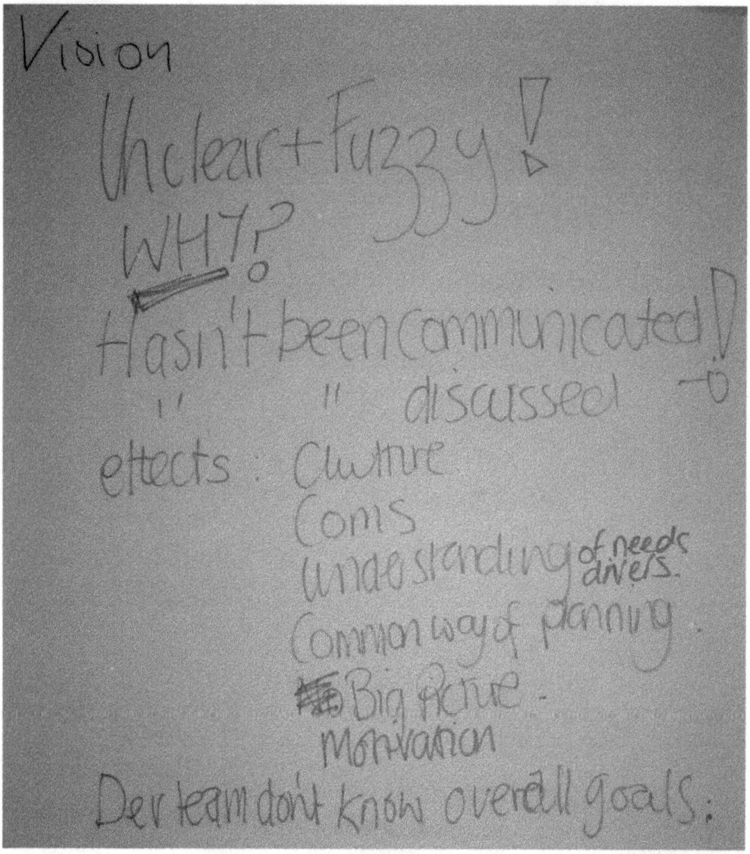

What will Solution

1) Define the Vision
   ↳ Steering Committee
   ↳ Sign off from strategic
              Board

2) Communicate - 15 second
                     sell
   ○ 1 pager to everyone in
                       team

                    to all stakeholders
   - longterm goal
   - motivation   → Goal hireachy
   - understanding
   ● Presentation - Sn P team
                    ↳cascade

3) Use the vision - everyone

Revisit the vision - steering comite

keep Presenting the vision
                    ↳ Sn B team

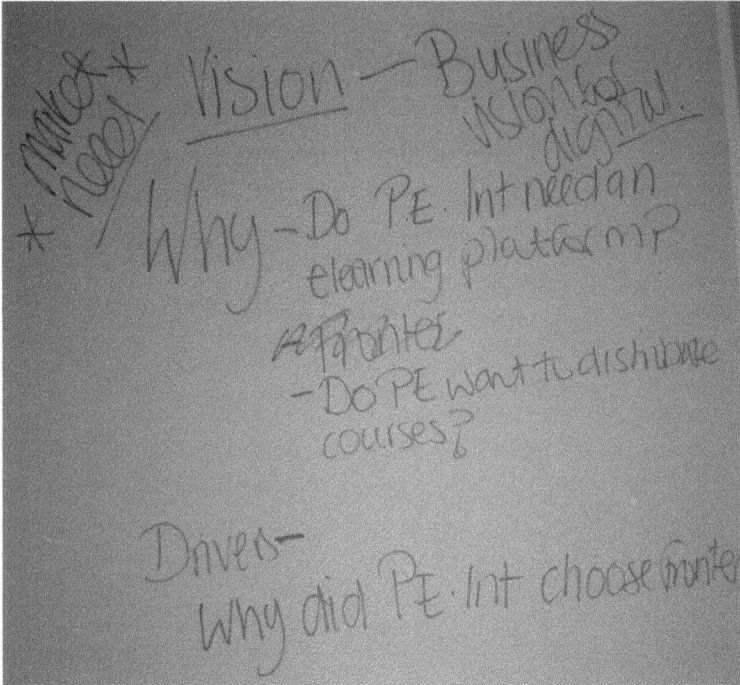

Also in terms of VISION the team decided to bring this to the awareness of the steering committee with the following expectations:

- Define a vision
- Communicate the vision to everyone in the team
- Use the vision

Planning

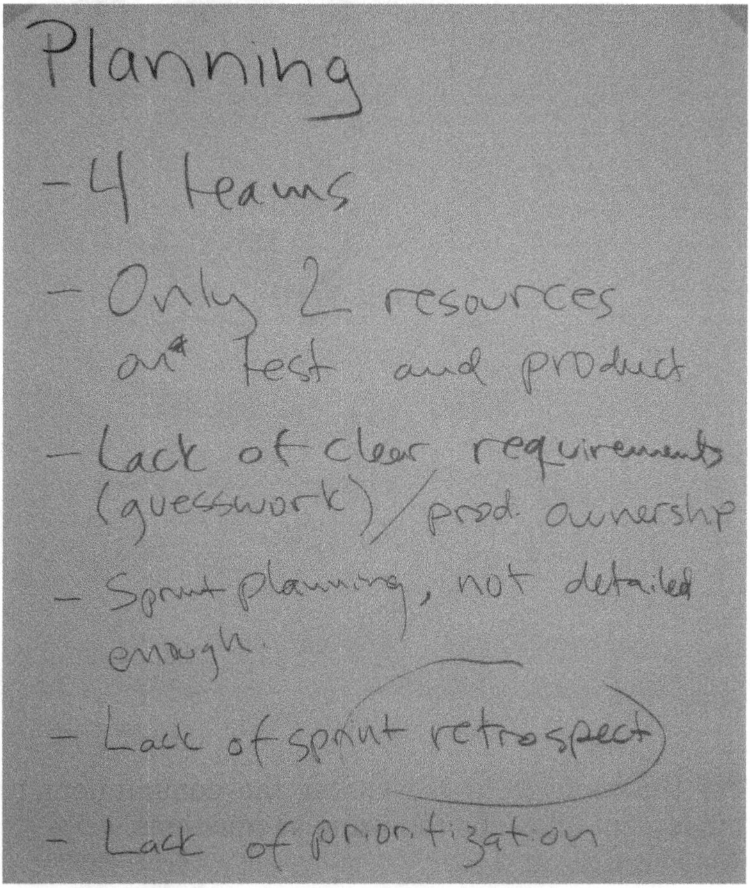

Planning

- 4 teams

- Only 2 resources on test and product

- Lack of clear requirements (guesswork) / prod. ownership

- Sprint planning, not detailed enough.

- Lack of sprint retrospect

- Lack of prioritization

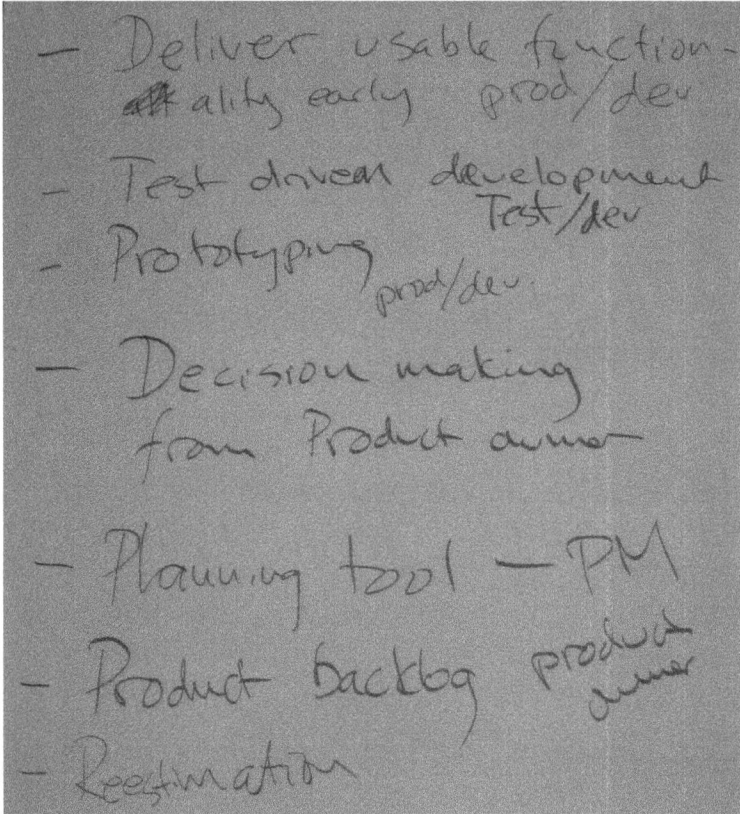

For the topic PLANNING was the commitment to implement all of the following suggestions:

- Deliver usable functionality early (prod/dev)
- Test driven development (test/dev)
- Prototyping (prod/dev)
- Decision making from Product Owner
- Planning tool (PM)
- Product backlog (PO)
- Re-estimation

Thank You!

Thank you for your open and honest comments and the concrete suggestions. I wish you success for the realization of your ideas in the next steps of the project!

Jutta Eckstein

About the Author

I hold a M.A. Business Coaching & Change Management, a Dipl.Eng. in Product-Engineering, and a B.A. in Education. Retrospective for Organizational Change was at the core of my master thesis.

I am working as an independent coach, consultant, and trainer. I have helped many teams and organizations all over the world to make the transition to an agile approach. I have a unique experience in applying agile processes within medium-sized to large distributed mission-critical projects. I focus also on techniques which help teach and learn and am a main lead in the pedagogical patterns project.

I am a member of the AgileAlliance[6] (having served on the board of directors from 2003-2007) and a member of the program committee of many different European, Asian, and American conferences, where I has also presented her work. At the last election, I have been designated for the Top 100 most important persons of the German IT.

If you liked this book, you might like the other books I've written:

- Co-authored with John Buck: Company-wide Agility with Beyond Budgeting, Open Space & Sociocracy: Survive & Thrive on Disruption[7]
- Agile Software Development with Distributed Teams: Staying Agile in a Global World[8]
- Agile Software Development in the Large: Diving into the Deep[9]
- Co-authored with Johanna Rothman: Diving for Hidden Treasures: Finding the Real Value in Your Project Portfolio[10]
- Pedagogical Patterns: Advice for Educators[11]

---

[6]http://agilealliance.org

[7]http://agilebossanova.com

[8]http://distributed-teams.com

[9]http://jeckstein.com/agilebook

[10]http://jeckstein.com/index.php/publications/diving-for-hidden-treasures

[11]http://jeckstein.com/pedagogical-patterns

Focusing mainly on the topic of company-wide agility, together with my co-author John Buck, I have a blog:

- BOSSA nova[12]

I'd like to stay in touch either through my web site[13] or via social media. Please do invite me to connect with you on LinkedIn[14] or on Xing[15].

I would love to know what you think of this book. If you write a review of it somewhere, please let me know. Thanks!

---

[12] http://www.agilebossanova.com/blog

[13] http://jeckstein.com

[14] http://de.linkedin.com/pub/jutta-eckstein/0/83/486

[15] http://www.xing.com/profile/Jutta_Eckstein

Other Books by the Authors

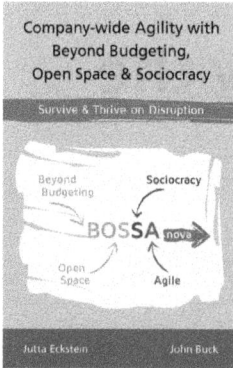

Company-wide Agility with Beyond Budgeting, Open Space & Sociocracy

Survive & Thrive on disruption

By Jutta Eckstein & John Buck

Today, companies are expected to be flexible and both rapidly responsive and resilient to change, which basically asks them to be agile. By combining Beyond Budgeting, Open Space, Sociocracy, and Agile, this book provides a practical guide for companies that want to be agile company-wide.

Enjoy insights in the book shared by Jez Humble, Diana Larsen, James Shore, Johanna Rothman, and Bjarte Bogsnes. Find out what Spotify, ING, Ericsson, and Walmart say in the book.

Quotes from early readers:

"[This is] a very important book. My hopes are that it will be the missing link between agile for teams and the flexible, adaptive and humane organisations we want to build. It's a great book. Thanks for writing it!" ~Sandy Mamoli, author of Creating Great Teams

"Just as Spotify has worked hard to make all aspects of product development align well and work together - I see Jutta and John in this book exploring methods and processes that will work very well across the whole company." ~ Anders Ivarsson, Spotify

"Company-wide Agility with Beyond Budgeting, Open Space and Sociocracy [...] makes an important case for companies to regard trust and autonomy the norm, rather than a privilege. [...] Overall a great overview of how leaders can reimagine the way power is distributed within their companies." ~ Aimee Groth, Author of The Kingdom of Happiness: Inside Tony Hsieh's Zapponian Utopia

This book invites you to take a new perspective that addresses the challenges of doing business in a volatile, uncertain, complex, and ambiguous world.

Diving for Hidden Treasures

Uncovering the Cost of Delay in Your Project Portfolio

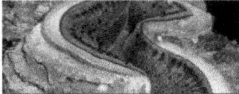

By Johanna Rothman & Jutta Eckstein

About the book:

Does your organization value and rank projects based on estimation? Except for the shortest projects, estimation is often wrong. You don't realize the value you planned when you wanted. How can you finish projects in time to realize their potential value?

Instead of estimation, consider using cost of delay to evaluate and rank projects. Cost of delay accounts for ways projects get stuck: multitasking, other projects not releasing on time, work queuing behind experts, excessive attention to code cleanliness, and management indecision to name several.

Once you know about cost of delay, you can decide what to do about it. You can stop the multitasking. You can eliminate the need for experts. You can reduce the number of projects and features in progress. You can use cost of delay to rank projects and work in your organization. Learn to use cost of delay to make better decisions for your project, program, or project portfolio.

Have you ever wondered about how your projects become late? Are you worried that your projects become later and you don't know why?

Cost of delay can tell you where the delays occur and why. Common practices, such as multitasking, experts, and even other projects' delay can make your project late. Learn simple tools and methods for analyzing and eliminating the costs of delay in your project.

Agile
Software
Development
with
Distributed Teams

Staying Agile in a Global World

by Jutta Eckstein

Agile Software Development with
Distributed Teams

Staying Agile in a Global World

By Jutta Eckstein

About the book:

All software projects face the challenges of diverse distances – temporal, geographical, cultural, lingual, political, historical, and more. Many forms of distance even affect developers in the same room. The goal of this book is to reconcile two mainstays of modern agility: the close collaboration agility relies on, and project teams distributed across different cities, countries, and continents.

In *Agile Software Development with Distributed Teams*, Jutta Eckstein asserts that, in fact, agile methods and the constant communication they require are uniquely capable of solving the challenges of distributed projects. Agility is responsiveness to change -- in other words, agile practitioners maintain flexibility to accommodate changing circumstances and results. Iterative development serves the learning curve that global project teams must scale.

This book is *not* about how to outsource and forget your problems. Rather, Eckstein details how to carefully select development partners and integrate efforts and processes to form a better product than any single contributor could deliver on his or her own. The author de-emphasizes templates and charts and favors topical discussion and exploration. Practitioners share experiences in their own words in short stories throughout the book. Eckstein trains readers to be change agents, to creatively apply the concepts in this book to form a customized distributed project plan for success.

Topics include:
• The Productivity Myth
• Ensuring Conceptual Integrity
• Trust and Mutual Respect
• Virtual Retrospectives

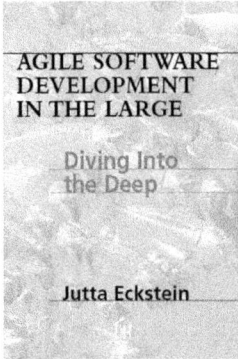

Agile Software Development in the Large

Diving into the Deep

By Jutta Eckstein

About the book:

Agile or "lightweight" processes have revolutionized the software development industry. They're faster and more efficient than traditional software development processes.

They enable developers to embrace requirement changes during the project, to deliver working software in frequent iterations, and moreover to focus on the human factor in software development.

Unfortunately, most agile processes are designed for small or mid-sized software development projects—bad news for large teams that have to deal with rapid changes to requirements. That means all large teams!

With *Agile Software Development in the Large*, Jutta Eckstein—a leading speaker and consultant in the agile community—shows how to scale agile processes to teams of up to 200. The same techniques are also relevant to teams of as few as 10 developers, especially within large organizations.

Topics include:
- the agile value system as used in large teams
- the impact of a switch to agile processes
- the agile coordination of several sub-teams
- the way project size and team size influence the underlying architecture

Stop getting frustrated with inflexible processes that cripple your large projects! Use this book to harness the efficiency and adaptability of agile software development.

Index

A

Action Learning, 25, 40–41
Action planning, 18
Action Review Cycle, 40–41
Adaptive Action, 25, 48, 50–52, 54–55
Agile Manifesto, 17, 61
Agile principles, 55
Agile software development, 4, 13, 53–54, 62–63
Agreement and certainty matrix, 27
Alignment, 24, 49
American Football, 11–12
Argyris and Schön, 21, 65
Attitude, 13–14, 33, 62

B

Beckhard & Pritchard, 23, 71
Big-picture, 16, 36, 42
Bogsnes, 29–30
Boy Scouts, 30
Bunker and Alban, 36
Butterfly Effect, 23, 39

C

Capacity building, 12, 66
Change, 1–2, 5, 7–8, 14, 21–28, 30, 33–43, 45–49, 52–55, 57–58, 60–63, 65–67, 69–71
Change Management, 1, 46, 48, 57, 66, 70
Church groups, 30
Classical retrospective, 33, 41, 43
Close the retrospective, 18
Collaboration, 4, 13, 33, 46, 63
Command-and-control, 29
Complex adaptive systems, 22, 46
Complex change, 24–25, 34, 57, 62, 69

Complexity, 13, 23, 25, 69
Continuous learning, 4–5, 12, 41, 63
Credibility attainment, 66
Culture, 15, 25, 62

D

Decide what to do, 18, 34, 43, 55, 59
Decision-making, 27, 29
Dedicated champion, 48
Democracy, 30
Derby, 4, 13, 17, 33, 38, 66
Diversity, 35, 41, 69
DNA, 37
Double-loop learning, 17, 25, 59, 66
Duration, 13
Dynamic change, 24–25, 34, 61
Dynamical change, 24

E

Eckstein, 2, 13
Eoyang, 22–23, 25, 37, 39, 48, 55, 65

F

Feedback, 2–4, 7, 11, 18, 45, 52, 54, 57, 63, 71
Finger-pointing, 15
Fractals, 37
Future pacing, 41
Futurespective, 40–42

G

Gather Data, 18, 34, 43, 48, 54–55
Generate Insights, 18, 43, 54, 59
Generation, 30, 42
Gladwell, 39
Gleick, 22–23
Graeßner, 3, 7–8, 58
Gratton, 8, 23, 29, 35
Gribbin, 39

H

Holladay, 23, 25–27, 39, 48, 55, 65
Holman, Devane, and Cady, 28, 35
Human Systems Dynamics, 48

I

Involvement, 29, 60, 66–67

K

Karten, 13–14
Kerth, 3, 13–16
Knapp, 69–70
Kotter, 21–22, 24, 40, 66
Kua, 41
Kurtz, 25

L

Landscape Diagram, 26–27, 34
Larsen, 4, 13, 17, 33, 38, 54, 66
Lateral, 30
Leadership, 24, 29, 66–67
Lewin, 21, 24
Lindberg, 22, 26–27

M

Manns, 48–49, 66

N

Now what, 49–51, 55

O

Open Space, 45, 57
Organizational Learning Cycle, 40, 42–43
organized zone, 27–28

P

Participation, 5, 13, 29–30, 35
Participative project management, 41
Personal development, 15
Plsek, 22, 26–27
Prime directive, 14–15, 33

R

Reflection, 12, 15, 18, 42, 65–66, 69
Resistance, 14, 48, 60
Retrospective phases, 17
Revans, 25, 40
RfG, 45–46, 48, 57, 71
Rifkin, 30
Rising, 48–49, 66

138

S

Same-and-Different, 55
Satir, 47, 49
Scharmer, 5, 12, 25, 37, 39, 52
Seifert, 17
Self-organizing zone, 27
Senge, 11, 15, 29, 34, 37, 42, 66
Set the Stage, 17
Single-loop learning, 17
Snowden, 25
So what, 49, 54
Stacey, 15, 26–27, 36, 59, 70
Static change, 23, 25, 34

T

Transparency, 30
Transparent, 30, 34, 50
Treadmill, 15

U

Unclear goals, 26
unorganized zone, 27

V

Vertical power, 30

W

What, 3, 5, 8, 13–16, 18, 21–23,
    28, 34–39, 42–43, 46, 48–52,
    54–55, 58–59, 61–62, 69, 71
Whitmore, 5, 14, 35
World Café, 59–60

Z

Zimmerman, 22, 26–27

www.ingramcontent.com/pod-product-compliance
Lightning Source LLC
Chambersburg PA
CBHW071659210326
41597CB00017B/2245